KIDNEY TRANSPLANT DIET COOKBOOK FOR SENIORS

The Simple And Satisfying Kidney-Conscious Recipes For Seniors To Thrive After Transplant

Kathleen Scribner

TABLE OF CONTENTS

INTRODUCTION

Overview of Kidney Transplant Diet

A kidney transplant is a life-altering procedure that gives elderly people a second opportunity at leading healthier, more active lives. Nonetheless, post-transplant care—particularly with regard to dietary decisions—is essential to guaranteeing the lifespan and effectiveness of the kidney transplant. This cookbook offers a thorough guidance to a nutritious and kidney-friendly diet and is designed especially for seniors who have had kidney transplants.

One of the most important aspects of geriatric kidney transplant treatment is proper diet. The objective is to preserve the functioning of the transplanted kidney in addition to promoting the person's general health and well-being. A well planned diet can assist in managing possible side effects, such as diabetes and high blood pressure, which are frequently linked to kidney transplants.

It's important to know the fundamentals of a diet after kidney transplantation. Seniors need to be aware of things like protein consumption, potassium, phosphorus, and salt levels. Maintaining good health and avoiding kidney strain requires balancing these components. This cookbook will help seniors navigate these nutritional issues by providing useful advice and mouth watering meals that are customized to meet their individual requirements.

After receiving a kidney transplant, seniors frequently have to adjust to a new food environment. Although this change might be daunting, it can be made bearable and productive with the correct information and assistance. The book will give seniors a road map for modifying their eating habits without compromising taste or diversity, stressing the value of little adjustments.
Beyond the physical factors, diet is essential for enabling seniors to actively participate in their own health care. The goal of this cookbook is to provide readers with information so they may make decisions that suit their own tastes and cultural norms. Through the process of deconstructing the

complexity of a diet after kidney transplant, seniors may now approach meals with self-assurance and inventiveness.

The kidney transplant diet is about adopting a whole-person approach to wellbeing, not simply about following rules. The book will focus on helping seniors have a healthy connection with food by including scrumptious and nutritious foods into their everyday routines. Every recipe, from breakfast to dessert, has been thoughtfully chosen to be both pleasant and kidney-friendly, guaranteeing seniors a gratifying and rewarding dining experience.

To sum up, this review lays the groundwork for the whole trip this cookbook provides seniors who have had kidney transplants. Through the integration of pragmatic observations, dietary recommendations, and an assortment of mouthwatering recipes, this book transforms into an essential tool for elderly individuals seeking to maintain their health and energy.

Importance of Nutrition for Seniors

When it comes to the treatment of patients following a kidney transplant, nutrition is a silent hero that has a huge impact on patients' recuperation, just like James. Let's explore the fascinating tale of James, a strong guy whose kidney transplant changed his life dramatically.

When James's kidneys started to fail, the 70-year-old retiree found himself in a difficult situation. The prognosis was evident: in order to restore his quality of life, a kidney transplant was required. Once he set out on this path, James soon found that his transplant's outcome depended as much on his nutritional decisions as it did on the surgeon's expertise.

James had to tackle the difficult challenge of acclimating to a new eating regimen in the first few weeks following his transplant. His medical staff made a strong impression on him on the significance of eating a healthy diet, explaining to him how certain nutrients were essential to both his recovery and the durability of his kidney transplant. James remembers clearly the first difficulties he had in figuring out the dietary maze that was in front of him. Sodium, potassium, and phosphorus were words that he used on a regular basis. James started to understand the nuances of a kidney-friendly diet with the help of his medical team and the information found in books like this one.

James saw an increase in energy and vitality when he adopted a diet high in foods high in nutrients and low in meals that stress the kidneys. It was about creating a lifestyle that fed his body and soul, not just about adhering to a set of rules. This cookbook's delectable meals became his traveling companions, demonstrating that eating a kidney-friendly diet could provide happiness and contentment.

James's tale serves as evidence of the positive impact that eating may have on seniors who have had kidney transplants. By making thoughtful decisions, he restored his sense of wellbeing and promoted the health of his transplanted kidney. This book's expertly created recipes let him enjoy tastes without sacrificing his health objectives.

Though there were ups and downs along the way, James's dedication to diet turned into a ray of optimism. His experience is consistent with the more general reality that nutrition is a dynamic force that may impact a person's health and vitality rather than just a collection of rules.

Let James's story serve as a potent reminder as we delve into this investigation of the kidney transplant diet for seniors: nutrition is more than simply a means of subsistence; it's a lifeline and an important factor in the incredible tales of recovery that emerge after transplant. The upcoming chapters will shed more light on the road to wellness by offering helpful advice and delectable recipes to help elders like James have meaningful lives.

CHAPTER ONE

UNDERSTANDING KIDNEY HEALTH

Basics of Kidney Function

Understanding the basic wonder of kidney function is crucial as we navigate the complexities of post-kidney transplant care. The two bean-shaped organs that are situated on either side of the spine, the kidneys, are essential to preserving general health. Let's deconstruct the amazing roles that these organs play, as we examine the fundamentals.

Filtration and Waste Removal

The amazing capacity of kidneys to filter blood is at the core of their function. These organs filter out around 2 quarts of waste and extra water from about 200 quarts of blood each day. Think of it as an intricate, precisely calibrated filtering system that makes sure the body doesn't contain any pollutants and keeps the fluid equilibrium in the body.

Regulating Blood Pressure

The kidneys play a crucial role in blood pressure regulation in addition to eliminating waste. The renin-angiotensin-aldosterone system, a complex system that modifies blood volume and affects blood vessel constriction, is how they accomplish this. For general cardiovascular health, seniors—especially those who have received a kidney transplant—benefit substantially from maintaining appropriate blood pressure levels.

Electrolyte Balance

The body's electrolyte balance, which includes sodium, potassium, and phosphorus, is expertly maintained by the kidneys. These minerals are necessary for many body processes, and the kidneys regulate their concentrations carefully. Seniors should monitor these electrolyte levels after transplantation since abnormalities may affect the functioning of the new kidney.

Erythropoiesis and Vitamin D Activation

Erythropoietin, which the kidneys secrete, aids in the synthesis of red blood cells. By encouraging the bone marrow to create red blood cells, this hormone makes sure that the body gets enough oxygen. Furthermore, vitamin D, which is essential for bone health and calcium absorption, is activated by the kidneys.

Comprehending these complex processes is essential to realizing the importance of the diet prescribed after kidney transplantation. Seniors who have had transplants should be aware of the need of maintaining these functions with a diet high in nutrients and balance.

Let us use this information as a starting point to guide our dietary decisions as we go deeper into our understanding of renal function. The first steps in achieving long-term wellbeing after a kidney transplant are realizing the wonders of these essential organs and understanding the part diet plays in maintaining their functionality and advancing general health.

Common Challenges After Kidney Transplant

While a kidney transplant is an important life event for seniors, it also brings with it a new set of difficulties that need to be carefully considered and managed proactively. Seniors who want to navigate the post-transplant world with perseverance and confidence must be aware of these frequent hurdles.

Immunosuppression and Infection Risks

Using immunosuppressive drugs is one of the main difficulties after a kidney transplant. These drugs suppress the immune system even though they are essential for keeping the body from rejecting the donated kidney. In order to reduce their risk of infection, seniors should avoid crowded areas, maintain current immunizations, and practice proper hygiene as advised by their healthcare provider.

Monitoring Medication and Side Effects

Seniors must follow a complicated drug schedule after receiving a donation. For the sake of avoiding rejection and preserving general health, consistency is essential. But given the possible adverse effects, this can be difficult. It is usual to have fluctuations in blood pressure, fatigue, and gastrointestinal problems. It's critical to have regular contact with medical professionals in order to resolve issues and improve prescription regimens.

Fluid and Electrolyte Balance

For seniors who have had kidney transplants, maintaining a delicate balance of fluids and electrolytes becomes a recurring concern. Even though the body's capacity to control these variables is greatly enhanced by the donated kidney, seniors still need to pay close attention to their hydration and electrolyte intake. This is especially significant when considering food choices and how they affect renal function.

Managing Chronic Conditions

Many elderly patients undergoing kidney transplants already suffer from chronic illnesses like diabetes or hypertension. A coordinated and individualized strategy is needed to address these problems while providing post-transplant care. Because health is interrelated, a comprehensive approach that takes into account several aspects of wellbeing is necessary.

Psychological and Emotional Well-being

For seniors, the post-transplant phase can be emotionally taxing. The stress of surgery and continuous lifestyle modifications aside, psychological wellness is essential to general health. Anxiety and despair are only two of the many emotions that may affect seniors. It takes a strong network of family and friends and the assistance of mental health specialists to overcome these obstacles.

With an exploration of the intricacies of living following a kidney transplant, this book seeks to offer useful advice and assistance to elderly individuals dealing with these typical difficulties. Every chapter is intended to provide seniors with information, techniques, and answers to improve their well-being while they embark on this life-changing adventure. Together, we'll look at strategies for overcoming setbacks and embracing a happy, full life after kidney transplantation.

CHAPTER TWO

NUTRITIONAL GUIDELINES

Recommended Nutrient Intake

An appropriately balanced diet promotes both general health and the lifetime of the transplanted organ, which is especially beneficial for seniors who have received a kidney transplant. Creating a diet plan that takes into account the particular requirements of people who have had transplants requires an understanding of the appropriate nutritional intake.

1. Protein: Finding the Correct Ratio

For seniors undergoing kidney transplants, protein is essential because it promotes immunological function and helps heal damaged tissue. On the other hand, consuming too much protein might cause renal strain. It is recommended that seniors eat modest portions of high-quality protein sources, such as fish, poultry, eggs, lean meats, and plant-based foods like tofu and beans. Vigilant observation, particularly in collaboration with medical professionals, guarantees equilibrium that fosters recovery without placing undue strain on the kidneys.

2. Sodium: Controlling Fluid Balance and Blood Pressure

For elders to maintain appropriate fluid balance and control blood pressure, salt consumption must be strictly limited. Due to the high salt content of processed and packaged meals, seniors should prioritize eating fresh, natural foods. Spices and herbs with flavor can be used in place of salt to improve the flavor of food without endangering kidney health.

3. Potassium: Achieving the Correct Amounts

Although potassium is necessary for many body processes, including nerve and muscle function, seniors who have had transplants should be aware of their potassium levels. Typical sources of potassium are some legumes, fruits, and vegetables. Modest potassium consumption should be incorporated into the diet to help avoid imbalances that can harm the transplanted kidney.

4. Phosphorus: Searching for Stealthy Entities

Many meals include phosphorus, which might be difficult for elderly people who have had transplants. Heart and bone problems can be exacerbated by an excess of phosphorus. Common sources include nuts, dairy products, and some processed meals. It is recommended that seniors consume less phosphorus and, whenever feasible, opt for low-phosphorus options. This methodical technique protects against any issues without compromising the diversity of nutrients.

5. Fluids: Managing Your Hydration

For elders receiving a kidney transplant, it's critical to maintain appropriate hydration. Although it's important to keep hydrated, consuming too much fluids might damage the kidneys. The advice of their healthcare team and their own requirements should be taken into consideration while monitoring and adjusting fluid consumption for seniors. Adding meals that are high in water content, including fruits and vegetables, also helps you stay hydrated overall.

6. Minerals and Vitamins: Vital to Health

Seniors who have had kidney transplants should make sure they are getting enough important vitamins and minerals. This contains calcium for general health, iron to avoid anemia, and vitamin D for strong bones. These vital needs are partially met by a well-balanced diet that consists of a range of nutrient-dense foods and, if needed, supplements taken under medical supervision.

The goal of this chapter is to provide seniors useful advice on reaching optimal nutritional intake so they may make decisions that will benefit their kidney transplant success as well as their overall health. Every suggestion we make as we delve into the gastronomic realm of post-transplant diet is designed to improve seniors' quality of life and promote a lifetime of wellbeing.

Dietary Restrictions for Kidney Transplant Recipients

Dietary restrictions are essential for kidney transplant recipients in order to protect the organ's health and function. Comprehending and honoring these limitations is one of the most important components of post-transplant treatment, guaranteeing a purposeful gastronomic journey that promotes general health.

1. Sodium: Controlling the Salinity

Consuming excessive amounts of salt can raise blood pressure, which can be dangerous for kidney transplant and cardiovascular health. Those who receive kidney transplants are recommended to consume less salt. This entails staying away from canned items, highly processed foods, and restaurant meals that are notorious for having a lot of salt. Using herbs and spices for taste and embracing fresh, complete foods makes cooking a fulfilling and health-promoting activity.

2. Potassium: Equilibrium Action

Although potassium is a necessary element, renal strain can result from high potassium levels. Patients receiving transplants should watch how much potassium they eat, particularly if their kidneys have trouble controlling this mineral. Foods high in potassium, such as oranges, bananas, and other vegetables, should be eaten in moderation. Tailored meal programs developed in association with medical specialists guarantee a well-rounded and kidney-friendly strategy.

3. Phosphorous: A Sensitive Bound

For kidney transplant recipients, phosphorus control is essential since elevated levels can aggravate cardiovascular and bone problems. Common sources of phosphorus are dairy products, nuts, and some processed meals. In order to maintain a delicate balance that promotes general health, seniors are recommended to restrict their consumption and opt for low-phosphorus alternatives.

4. Fluid Intake: Finding equilibrium

It's crucial for kidney transplant recipients to be properly hydrated, but they also need to find a balance so as not to overtax their kidneys. It becomes proactive to monitor hydration consumption depending on personal requirements and medical guidance. A balanced approach to hydration includes hydrating meals, mindfully drinking throughout the day, and modifying fluid consumption based on lifestyle and weather circumstances.

5. Protein: Value Is Greater Than Amount

Although protein is necessary for immune system and tissue repair, consuming too much of it might damage the kidneys. It is recommended that patients of kidney transplants take modest quantities of high-quality protein from plant-based foods, lean meats, fish, and eggs. Protein consumption should be customized to each patient's needs under the direction of medical professionals to guarantee a balance that promotes healing without overstressing the kidneys.

6. Restricting Fruits and Vegetables High in Potassium

A balanced diet must include fruits and vegetables, however kidney transplant recipients may need to restrict high-potassium fruits and vegetables. Finding a balance between potassium management and nutritional advantages can be achieved by collaborating with healthcare specialists to identify and regulate the intake of particular fruits and vegetables.

Recipients of kidney transplants who comprehend and accept these dietary limitations are more equipped to actively participate in their post-transplant care. This chapter acts as a manual, offering helpful advice and methods for making deliberate culinary decisions. Recipients lay the groundwork for long-term kidney transplant success and maintained health by adopting these dietary limitations into their everyday lives.

CHAPTER THREE

MEAL PLANNING FOR SENIORS

Balanced Meal Principles

Seniors who have had a kidney transplant greatly benefit from following balanced eating guidelines, which enhance general health and prolong the life of the donated organ. The development of nutritious plates customized to meet the unique requirements of people who have had transplants is guided by the following concepts.

1. Variety of Protein Sources: Foundational Elements for Well-Being

Every meal should include a range of lean protein sources. Without overtaxing the kidneys, foods including fish, chicken, eggs, tofu, and legumes offer the vital amino acids needed for tissue regeneration. This idea guarantees a balanced nutritional profile while reducing stress on the kidney that has been transplanted.

2. Vibrant, Nutrient-Rich Vegetables: The Abundance of Nature

To optimize nutritional intake, pile a rainbow of veggies onto the plate. Select a range of hues to represent different minerals and vitamins. Vegetables like broccoli, bell peppers, and cauliflower are high in fiber and antioxidants, but watch the potassium intake. These foods are also good for your health.

3. Regulated Amounts: Astute and Fulfilling

To reduce calorie intake and avoid overtaxing the digestive system, practice portion management. Seniors who have received a kidney transplant should strive for balanced meals that provide them prolonged energy without going overboard. A balanced and fulfilling meal experience may be achieved by estimating servings, using smaller plates, and paying attention to your body's signals of hunger and fullness.

4. Whole Grains: The Energy Basis

For long-lasting energy and vital nutrients, choose whole grains like brown rice, quinoa, and whole wheat bread. Whole grains can be a part of a well-rounded food plan for seniors who have had kidney transplants. They are high in fiber, which supports digestive health.

5. Nutritious Fats: Filling from the Inside Out

To promote heart health and satiety, include foods high in healthy fats, such as nuts, avocados, and olive oil. Even though it's best to limit fat intake, adding these nutrient-dense sources to meals improves their flavor and nutritional value for elderly citizens.

6. Smart Selections: Minimize Processed and High-Sodium Foods

Reduce your intake of processed and high-sodium foods in order to preserve renal and blood pressure health. Seniors may better manage the components in their meals and adhere to the principles of a kidney-friendly diet by cooking at home and selecting fresh, whole foods.

7. Hydration: An Essential Component

Make being hydrated a priority by eating meals high in water, such fruits and vegetables, and making sure you are getting enough fluids throughout the day. While taking into account fluid limitations, maintaining enough hydration promotes kidney function and general health.

Seniors who have had kidney transplants should use these balanced meal concepts as a guide to make healthy decisions that support long-term health. Seniors who adopt these ideas provide the groundwork for long-term wellbeing and promote a happy and satisfying post-transplant journey.

Portion Control Tips

A key component of post-kidney transplant diet is portion management, which helps seniors find the ideal balance between meeting their nutritional requirements and not overtaxing their newly donated kidneys. The following advice helps seniors choose meal proportions that will promote their health.

1. Use Tinier Bowls and Plates: Considerate Serving Sizes

Choosing smaller bowls and plates can help to naturally control portion sizes. This visual cue encourages attentive eating and discourages overindulging by making you feel satisfied with less food.

2. Recognize Cues of Hunger and Fullness: Pay Attention to Your Body

Recognize the signs of hunger and fullness sent by your body. Savor every bite as you eat slowly, pausing in between to gauge how full you are. This attentive method encourages a better connection with food and helps avoid overindulging.

3. Measure Parts: Moderate Precision

To precisely measure portion sizes, use a food scale, measuring cups, or spoons. This accuracy guarantees that you are getting the nutrients you need without accidentally going over suggested limits, particularly when it comes to important areas like salt and protein consumption.

4. Prioritize Nutrient Density Over Quantity

Give top priority to foods that are high in vitamins, minerals, and other vital nutrients per serving. This enables older citizens to get the most out of their diet without consuming excessive amounts of calories or fat. Good sources of nutrients include fruits, vegetables, lean meats, and whole grains.

5. Eat Larger Meals Together: Having Fun Socially

Think about splitting larger portions with a buddy or family member while cooking at home or dining out. This encourages a good and pleasurable mealtime experience by supporting portion management and enhancing the social component of meals.

6. Pre-portion Snacks: Intentionally Snack

Preparing food in advance is essential. Consider dividing snacks into smaller containers or buying pre-packaged single portions rather than eating straight from a huge bag. This approach facilitates greater control over portion amounts and helps avoid mindless eating.

7. Pay Attention to Liquid Calorie: Drink Caution

Be mindful of the calories in liquids, such as drinks and soups. Choose low-calorie beverages like water, herbal teas, and other drinks to remain hydrated without consuming too many calories. Pick broth-based soups that emphasize veggies and lean meats while you're eating them.

8. Make Equilibrated Plates: Measurements Count

Aim for well-balanced meals that feature different food categories in the right amounts. This might entail setting aside portions of your meal for nutritious grains, lean meats, and veggies. You may naturally regulate portion sizes and maintain a well-rounded nutritional profile by visually organizing your meals.

Seniors who have had kidney transplants may sustain a healthy balance between enjoying fulfilling meals and extending the life of their donated kidneys by implementing these portion management suggestions into their everyday lives. With the help of these doable techniques, seniors may confidently manage portion sizes and promote a healthy, long-term approach to post-transplant nutrition.

CHAPTER FOUR

KIDNEY-FRIENDLY RECIPES
FOR SENIORS

Delicious Breakfast Delights
For Seniors

1. Berry Bliss Smoothie Bowl

Ingredients:

- 1/2 cup mixed berries (such as strawberries, blueberries, and raspberries), frozen
- 1/2 ripe banana, frozen
- 1/4 cup plain Greek yogurt (low-fat or non-fat)
- 1/4 cup unsweetened almond milk (or any milk of choice)
- 1 tablespoon chia seeds
- 1 tablespoon honey (optional)

- **Toppings:** sliced strawberries, blueberries, raspberries, granola, sliced almonds, shredded coconut

Instructions:

1. Put the frozen banana, Greek yogurt, chia seeds, almond milk, mixed berries, and honey (if using) in a blender.
2. Blend until creamy and smooth, adding extra almond milk as necessary to get the right consistency.
3. Transfer the blended drink to a bowl.
4. You may add granola, sliced almonds, shredded coconut, strawberries, blueberries, raspberries, or any other toppings you choose on top.
5. Present right away and savor with a spoon.

2. Vegetable and Feta Omelette

Ingredients:

- 2 large eggs
- 1/4 cup low-fat feta cheese, crumbled
- 1/4 cup bell peppers, diced
- 1/4 cup zucchini, diced
- 1/4 cup cherry tomatoes, halved

- 1 tablespoon olive oil
- 1 tablespoon fresh parsley, chopped (optional)
- Salt and pepper to taste

Instructions:

1. Beat the eggs well in a basin. Add a dash of pepper and salt for seasoning.
2. In a nonstick skillet, warm the olive oil over medium heat.
3. Include cherry tomatoes, zucchini, and bell peppers in the skillet. Vegetables should be sautéed until soft but not cooked through.
4. Evenly divide the whisked eggs onto the cooked veggies by pouring them over them.
5. Top the eggs with crumbled feta cheese.
6. Cook the omelet for a few minutes without moving, or until the edges are firm.
7. To allow any egg that isn't cooked to flow to the edges, tilt the pan and gently raise the edges with a spatula.
8. Using the spatula, fold the omelet in half once it has set mostly.
9. Cook the omelet for a minute more, or until the cheese melts and it is well cooked.
10. If preferred, garnish with fresh parsley and serve.

3. Whole Grain Pancakes with Fresh Fruit Topping

Ingredients:

- 1 cup whole wheat flour
- 1 tablespoon baking powder
- 1 tablespoon sugar (optional)
- 1/4 teaspoon salt
- 1 egg
- 1 cup low-fat milk or unsweetened almond milk
- 2 tablespoons vegetable oil or melted butter
- Fresh fruit topping: sliced strawberries, blueberries, bananas, or any fruit of choice
- Maple syrup or honey (optional)

Instructions:

1. Combine the whole wheat flour, baking powder, salt, and sugar (if using) in a large basin.
2. Beat the egg in another basin and mix in the milk and vegetable oil (or melted butter).
3. Add the wet mixture to the dry mixture and whisk just until blended. Avoid overmixing; a little lumpiness in the batter is OK.
4. Turn up the heat to medium on a nonstick skillet or griddle. Apply a tiny bit of oil or cooking spray as a light grease.

5. For each pancake, add around 1/4 cup of batter to the skillet. Cook until the edges start to firm and bubbles appear on the surface, then turn and continue cooking until the other side is golden brown.

6. Continue with the leftover batter, reducing the heat as needed to avoid burning.

7. Top the steaming pancakes with pieces of fresh fruit and, if preferred, a drizzle of honey or maple syrup.

4. Greek Yogurt Parfait with Nuts and Honey

Ingredients:

- 1 cup low-fat Greek yogurt
- 2 tablespoons chopped almonds or walnuts (choose lower phosphorus nuts)
- 1 tablespoon honey
- 1/4 cup fresh berries (blueberries or strawberries work well)
- 1 tablespoon ground flaxseeds (optional)
- 1/2 teaspoon vanilla extract (optional)

Instructions:

1. Spoon a layer of Greek yogurt into the bottom of a serving glass or dish.

2. Top the yogurt with a layer of fresh berries.

3. Top the berries with chopped almonds.

4. Pour honey on top of the fruit and almonds.

5. Continue layering until you reach the top, then sprinkle more honey on top.

6. For added taste, feel free to add a small amount of vanilla essence.

7. For extra nutritious advantages, if preferred, top with ground flaxseeds.

8. Serve right away and savor this tasty and kidney-friendly Greek yogurt parfait!

5. *Avocado Toast with Poached Egg*

Ingredients:

- 1 ripe avocado
- 2 slices whole grain bread, toasted
- 2 large eggs
- Salt and pepper to taste
- **Optional toppings:** sliced cherry tomatoes, chopped fresh herbs (such as parsley or chives), red pepper flakes

Instructions:

1. To begin, poach the eggs. Pour some water into a small pot and heat it gently over medium heat.

2. Crack each egg into a ramekin or little dish. Gently place every egg into the water that is simmering. For a soft yolk, cook for 3–4 minutes, or longer if preferred.

3. Cut the avocado in halves and remove the pit while the eggs are poaching. Place the avocado flesh in a bowl and use a fork to mash it until it's smooth. To taste, add salt and pepper for seasoning.

4. Evenly distribute the mashed avocado over the slices of toasted whole grain bread.

5. After the eggs have finished poaching, use a slotted spoon to carefully remove them from the water and drain any extra water.

6. Top each avocado toast with one poached egg.

7. If preferred, garnish with extras like red pepper flakes, chopped fresh herbs, or sliced cherry tomatoes.

8. While the eggs are still warm, serve right away.

6. Cottage Cheese and Pineapple Stuffed Crepes

Ingredients:

For the Crepes:

- 1 cup all-purpose flour
- 1 1/2 cups low-fat milk
- 2 large eggs
- 1 tablespoon melted unsalted butter
- 1/4 teaspoon salt

For the Filling:

- 1 cup low-fat cottage cheese
- 1/2 cup pineapple chunks (fresh or canned in juice, drained)
- 1 tablespoon honey
- 1/4 teaspoon vanilla extract (optional)

For Garnish:

- Fresh mint leaves (optional)
- Additional pineapple chunks

Instructions:

For the Crepes:

1. Put the flour, milk, eggs, melted butter, and salt in a blender. Process till smooth.

2. Turn up the heat to medium and give a non-stick skillet a quick coat of cooking spray or a little butter.

3. Swirl a tiny quantity of batter into the skillet to equally coat the bottom. Cook for a few minutes until the edges begin to rise, then turn and continue cooking. Continue until the batter is all utilized.

For the Filling:

1. Combine cottage cheese, honey, pineapple chunks, and vanilla essence (if using) in a bowl. Mix well until fully incorporated.

Assembly:

1. On a level surface, spread out a crepe.

2. Spoon one side of the crepe with a large amount of the cottage cheese and pineapple filling.

3. To form a half-moon shape, fold the remaining half over the filling.

4. Continue with the remaining filling and crepes.

Garnish:

1. If preferred, garnish the packed crepes with fresh mint leaves.

2. Present more pineapple pieces alongside.

7. Sweet Potato and Spinach Breakfast Hash

Ingredients:

- 2 medium sweet potatoes, peeled and diced
- 1 tablespoon olive oil
- 1 small onion, diced
- 2 cloves garlic, minced
- 2 cups fresh spinach leaves, roughly chopped
- Salt and pepper to taste
- **Optional seasonings:** paprika, cumin, thyme
- **Optional toppings:** poached or fried eggs, chopped fresh parsley or green onions

Instructions:

1. In a big pan over medium heat, warm the olive oil.
2. Add the diced sweet potatoes to the skillet and cook for 10 to 12 minutes, turning periodically, or until they are soft and golden brown.
3. When the onion is transparent and softened, add the chopped onion to the skillet and cook for a further three to four minutes.
4. Add the minced garlic and stir until fragrant, about 1 more minute.

5. Add the chopped spinach to the skillet and heat it, turning now and again, until the spinach wilts and shrinks in size.

6. Add salt, pepper, and any more extra ingredients to taste when preparing the hash. Toss to blend thoroughly.

7. Cook for a few more minutes, or until all of the ingredients are well cooked and blended.

8. Present the hot Sweet Potato and Spinach Breakfast Hash, with the option to garnish it with fried or poached eggs and finely chopped green onions or fresh parsley.

8. Chia Seed Pudding with Berries

Ingredients:

- 1/4 cup chia seeds
- 1 cup low-fat milk (or a milk substitute like almond milk)
- 1 tablespoon honey or maple syrup
- 1/2 teaspoon vanilla extract
- A pinch of salt
- 1/2 cup mixed berries (blueberries, strawberries, raspberries)

Instructions:

1. Put the low-fat milk, vanilla essence, honey (or maple syrup), chia seeds, and a small amount of salt in a bowl.

2. In order to prevent clumping, carefully whisk the ingredients together.

3. After letting the mixture settle for about five minutes, whisk it once more to remove any remaining chia seed clusters.

4. To enable the chia seeds to absorb the liquid and take on the consistency of pudding, cover the bowl and refrigerate for at least three hours or overnight.

5. To achieve a uniform texture before serving, mix the chia pudding.

6. Ladle the chia pudding into glasses or serving dishes.

7. Sprinkle mixed berries over the pudding.

9. Quinoa Breakfast Bowl with Almonds and Berries

Ingredients:

- 1/2 cup quinoa, rinsed
- 1 cup water or low-sodium vegetable broth
- 1/4 teaspoon cinnamon
- 1/4 cup sliced almonds

- 1/2 cup mixed berries (such as strawberries, blueberries, and raspberries)
- 1 tablespoon honey or maple syrup (optional)
- Greek yogurt or almond milk for serving (optional)

Instructions:

1. Put the quinoa, cinnamon, and water or vegetable broth in a small pot. After bringing to a boil, lower the heat to a simmer, cover, and cook the quinoa for 15 to 20 minutes, or until it is tender and the liquid has been absorbed.
2. Use a fork to fluff the cooked quinoa and let it cool slightly.
3. Spoon the cooked quinoa into dishes for dishing.
4. Place mixed berries and sliced almonds on top of each bowl.
5. For extra sweetness, drizzle with honey or maple syrup, if preferred.
6. You may top the Quinoa Breakfast Bowl with almond milk or Greek yogurt, if you'd like.

10. Smoked Salmon and Cream Cheese Bagel

Ingredients:

- 1 whole grain bagel, sliced and toasted
- 2-3 ounces smoked salmon
- 2 tablespoons low-fat cream cheese
- 1 tablespoon capers, drained
- 1 tablespoon diced red onion
- Fresh lemon slices
- Fresh dill, for garnish (optional)

Instructions:

1. Evenly spread each half of the toasted whole grain bagel with low-fat cream cheese.
2. Top the cream cheese with the pieces of smoked salmon.
3. Top the smoked salmon with a sprinkle of chopped red onion and capers.
4. Add some freshly squeezed lemon juice to the toppings.
5. If preferred, garnish with fresh dill.
6. Enjoy your Cream Cheese Bagel with Smoked Salmon immediately.

11. Banana Walnut Muffins

Ingredients:

- 1 1/2 cups whole wheat flour
- 1 teaspoon baking powder
- 1/2 teaspoon baking soda
- 1/4 teaspoon salt
- 3 ripe bananas, mashed
- 1/4 cup honey or maple syrup
- 1/4 cup unsweetened applesauce
- 1/4 cup low-fat milk or unsweetened almond milk
- 1 teaspoon vanilla extract
- 1/2 cup chopped walnuts

Instructions:

1. Set the oven temperature to 175°C, or 350°F. Grease or use paper liners to line a muffin pan.
2. Combine the whole wheat flour, baking soda, baking powder, and salt in a large basin.
3. In a separate dish, thoroughly blend the mashed bananas, milk, applesauce, honey or maple syrup, and vanilla extract.
4. Add the liquid mixture to the dry mixture and whisk just until blended. Avoid over-mixing.
5. Fold in the chopped walnuts gently.
6. Evenly distribute the batter into each muffin cup, filling them approximately two-thirds of the way.
7. Cook for eighteen to twenty minutes, or until a toothpick inserted into the middle of a muffin comes out clean.

8. After letting the muffins cool in the pan for a few minutes, move them to a wire rack to finish cooling.

12. Spinach and Mushroom Breakfast Quesadilla

Ingredients:

- 2 whole wheat or low-sodium tortillas
- 1 cup fresh spinach, chopped
- 1/2 cup mushrooms, sliced
- 1/4 cup low-fat shredded mozzarella cheese
- 2 large eggs, scrambled
- 1 tablespoon olive oil
- Salt and pepper to taste
- Salsa for serving (optional)

Instructions:

1. Heat the olive oil in a skillet over medium heat.
2. Fill the pan with chopped spinach and sliced mushrooms. Cook the veggies until they are tender and any extra liquid is gone by sautéing them.
3. To taste, add salt and pepper to the veggies.
4. Push the veggies to one side of the skillet and fill the empty space with the scrambled eggs.

5. Cook the eggs until they are well cooked, stirring now and again.

6. Add the scrambled eggs to the pan along with the cooked veggies.

7. Spoon half of the egg and veggie mixture over one tortilla that has been laid out in the pan.

8. Distribute half of the mozzarella cheese shreds evenly throughout the egg mixture.

9. Using a spatula to gently press down, place the second tortilla on top.

10. Cook for a few minutes on each side, or until the cheese has melted and the tortilla is brown.

11. Proceed with the second quesadilla in the same manner.

12. If you'd like, cut the quesadillas into wedges and serve them with salsa.

13. Mango and Coconut Overnight Oats

Ingredients:

- 1/2 cup rolled oats
- 1/2 cup unsweetened coconut milk (or any milk of choice)
- 1/4 cup plain Greek yogurt (low-fat or non-fat)
- 1/2 ripe mango, diced

- 2 tablespoons unsweetened shredded coconut
- 1 tablespoon honey or maple syrup (optional)
- Optional toppings: additional diced mango, toasted coconut flakes

Instructions:

1. Place the rolled oats, Greek yogurt, chopped mango, shredded coconut, coconut milk, and honey or maple syrup (if using) in a mason jar or other lidded container. Mix well to blend.
2. To help the oats soften and the flavors combine, cover the jar or container with the lid and chill it for at least 4 hours or overnight.
3. Give the overnight oats a nice toss before serving. You may adjust the consistency by adding a little amount of milk if the mixture is too thick.
4. If preferred, top the chilled Mango and Coconut Overnight Oats with more chopped mango and toasted coconut flakes.

14. Egg and Spinach Breakfast Sandwich

Ingredients:

- 1 whole wheat English muffin, toasted

- 1 large egg, cooked (you can prepare it as you prefer, such as fried, scrambled, or poached)
- 1/2 cup fresh spinach leaves
- 1 slice low-fat cheese (optional)
- Salt and pepper to taste
- 1 teaspoon olive oil or cooking spray

Instructions:

1. Heat cooking spray or olive oil in a skillet over medium heat.
2. Season the egg with salt and pepper and cook it according to your liking (fried, scrambled, or poached).
3. To slightly melt a slice of low-fat cheese, if using, lay it on top of the fried egg.
4. Arrange a layer of fresh spinach leaves on the toasted English muffin.
5. Top the spinach with the cooked egg, either with or without cheese.
6. Place the remaining English muffin half on top.
7. Gently press the sandwich to help the ingredients bind together.
8. Present right away.

15. Protein-Packed Green Smoothie

Ingredients:

- 1 cup fresh spinach leaves
- 1/2 cup cucumber, peeled and sliced
- 1/2 banana (use a small banana for lower potassium content)
- 1/2 cup low-fat Greek yogurt
- 1/2 cup almond milk (or any milk substitute)
- 1 tablespoon chia seeds
- 1 tablespoon almond butter (or sunflower seed butter for lower phosphorus)
- Ice cubes (optional)

Instructions:

1. Put the banana, low-fat Greek yogurt, almond milk, chia seeds, almond butter, fresh spinach, cucumber, and banana in a blender.
2. Blend until creamy and smooth. To get the right consistency, you can add additional almond milk if the smoothie is too thick.
3. To make the smoothie cooler, feel free to add ice cubes.
4. Transfer the smoothie into a glass and sip it right away.

Mouthwatering Lunch Recipes
For Seniors

1. Grilled Chicken Salad with Fresh Berries

Ingredients:

- 2 boneless, skinless chicken breasts
- Salt and pepper to taste
- 6 cups mixed salad greens (such as spinach, arugula, and romaine)
- 1 cup mixed fresh berries (such as strawberries, blueberries, and raspberries)
- 1/4 cup sliced almonds, toasted
- 1/4 cup crumbled feta cheese (optional)
- Balsamic vinaigrette dressing (homemade or store-bought), to taste

Instructions:

1. Turn the heat up to medium-high on your grill.
2. To taste, add salt and pepper to the chicken breasts.
3. Cook the chicken breasts on the grill for 6 to 8 minutes on each side, or until they are cooked through and no longer have a pink core. Depending on the thickness of the chicken breasts, cooking times might change. After they are done, take them from the grill and give them some time to rest before slicing.
4. Combine the mixed salad greens, sliced almonds, and a variety of fresh berries in a big bowl.
5. After grilling, cut the chicken breasts into slices and place them over the salad.

6. Top the salad with the crumbled feta cheese, if using.

7. Toss the salad gently to coat after adding a drizzle of balsamic vinaigrette dressing, to taste.

8. Enjoy your Grilled Chicken Salad with Fresh Berries right away after serving.

2. Vegetarian Stuffed Bell Peppers

Ingredients:

- 4 large bell peppers, halved and seeds removed
- 1 cup quinoa, cooked
- 1 can (15 oz) low-sodium black beans, drained and rinsed
- 1 cup corn kernels (fresh or frozen)
- 1 cup cherry tomatoes, diced
- 1/2 cup red onion, finely chopped
- 1/2 cup fresh cilantro, chopped
- 1 teaspoon ground cumin
- 1 teaspoon chili powder
- 1/2 teaspoon garlic powder
- 1 cup low-fat shredded cheese (cheddar or Mexican blend)
- Salt and pepper to taste
- Olive oil for drizzling

Instructions:

1. Turn the oven on to 375°F, or 190°C.
2. The cooked quinoa, black beans, corn, cherry tomatoes, red onion, cilantro, cumin, chili powder, garlic powder, salt, and pepper should all be combined in a big bowl.
3. Thoroughly blend the ingredients together.
4. Transfer the bell peppers, cut in half, to a baking dish.
5. Fill each pepper half with a spoonful of the quinoa and veggie mixture.
6. Sprinkle some shredded cheese on top of every filled pepper.
7. For more moisture, drizzle a little olive oil on top.
8. Bake the peppers for 25 to 30 minutes, or until they are soft, while covering the oven dish with foil.
9. Take off the foil and bake the cheese for a further five to ten minutes, or until it melts and starts to become brown.
10. Take them out of the oven, give them a little time to cool, and then serve.

3. Salmon and Quinoa Bowl with Roasted Vegetables

Ingredients:

- 2 salmon filets
- 1 cup quinoa, rinsed
- 2 cups mixed vegetables (such as bell peppers, zucchini, cherry tomatoes, and red onion), chopped
- 2 tablespoons olive oil
- Salt and pepper to taste
- 1 teaspoon dried herbs (such as thyme, rosemary, or oregano)
- Lemon wedges for serving
- Optional garnish: chopped fresh parsley or green onions

Instructions:

1. Set the oven temperature to 400°F, or 200°C.
2. Arrange the salmon filets on a parchment paper-lined baking sheet. Add some salt, pepper, and lemon juice for seasoning.
3. Evenly cover the mixed veggies in a separate baking sheet with a mixture of olive oil, salt, pepper, and dry herbs.
4. Roast the veggies and salmon in the oven for 15 to 20 minutes, or until the vegetables are soft and have a hint of caramelization and the salmon is cooked through and flakes easily with a fork.
5. Prepare the quinoa per the directions on the box and simmer it while the salmon and veggies roast.

This usually entails boiling two cups of water, adding the quinoa, lowering the heat, covering, and simmering the mixture until the water is absorbed and the quinoa is fluffy, typically fifteen minutes.

6. After everything is done, divide the cooked quinoa, roasted veggies, and salmon filets among serving dishes to create your bowls.

7. Add optional chopped green onions or fresh parsley as a garnish, and serve with lemon wedges on the side.

4. Mushroom and Spinach Frittata

Ingredients:

- 6 large eggs- 1 cup fresh spinach leaves, chopped
- 1 cup mushrooms, sliced
- 1/2 cup low-fat feta cheese, crumbled
- 1/4 cup red onion, finely chopped
- 1 clove garlic, minced
- 1 tablespoon olive oil
- Salt and pepper to taste
- Fresh herbs for garnish (such as parsley or chives)

Instructions:

1. Turn the oven on to 375°F, or 190°C.

2. Beat the eggs well in a basin. Add pepper and salt for seasoning.

3. In an oven-safe skillet, preheat the olive oil over medium heat.

4. Fill the pan with minced garlic and finely chopped red onion. Sauté the food until it becomes tender.

5. Place the sliced mushrooms in the skillet and heat them through, releasing their moisture and turning soft.

6. Add the chopped spinach and heat, stirring, until it wilts.

7. Cover the veggies in the skillet with the beaten eggs.

8. Evenly distribute the feta cheese crumbles on top of the egg mixture.

9. Cook until the edges firm, a few minutes on the heat.

10. Place the pan in the oven that has been warmed, and bake for 15 to 20 minutes, or until the frittata is set through.

11. After cooking, take it out of the oven and give it some time to cool.

12. Cut into wedges and garnish with fresh herbs.

5. *Mediterranean Chickpea Wrap*

Ingredients:

- 1 whole wheat or low-sodium wrap
- 1/2 cup canned chickpeas, drained and rinsed
- 1 tablespoon olive oil
- 1 clove garlic, minced
- 1/2 teaspoon ground cumin
- 1/2 teaspoon paprika
- Salt and pepper to taste
- 2 tablespoons hummus
- 1/4 cup cucumber, thinly sliced
- 1/4 cup cherry tomatoes, halved
- 1/4 cup red bell pepper, thinly sliced
- 2 tablespoons Kalamata olives, sliced
- 1/4 cup feta cheese, crumbled
- Fresh parsley for garnish (optional)
- Lemon wedges for serving

Instructions:

1. Heat the olive oil in a skillet over medium heat.
2. Once aromatic, add the minced garlic and sauté it for one minute.
3. Fill the skillet with the chickpeas, paprika, ground cumin, salt, and pepper. Cook until chickpeas are brown and spice-coated, about 5 to 7 minutes.
4. Follow the directions on the package to reheat the wrap.

5. Evenly cover the middle of the wrap with hummus.

6. Spoon the hummus into the seasoned chickpeas.

7. Arrange the chopped feta cheese, cherry tomatoes, red bell pepper, cucumber slices, and Kalamata olives on top of the chickpeas.

8. If preferred, garnish with fresh parsley.

9. Tightly roll the wrap by folding its sides.

10. Halve the wrapper lengthwise and present it with lemon wedges beside it.

6. Shrimp Stir-Fry with Brown Rice

Ingredients:

- 1 pound shrimp, peeled and deveined
- 2 cups cooked brown rice
- 2 cups mixed vegetables (such as bell peppers, broccoli, snap peas, carrots), chopped
- 2 tablespoons low-sodium soy sauce
- 1 tablespoon sesame oil
- 2 cloves garlic, minced
- 1 teaspoon ginger, grated
- 2 tablespoons olive oil or vegetable oil
- **Optional garnish:** sliced green onions, sesame seeds

Instructions:

1. In a large skillet or wok, heat one tablespoon of vegetable or olive oil over medium-high heat.
2. Cook the grated ginger and minced garlic in the pan for approximately a minute, or until fragrant.
3. When the mixed veggies are crisp-tender, add them to the pan and stir-fry for three to four minutes.
4. Push the veggies to one side of the skillet and coat the empty side with the last tablespoon of oil.
5. When the shrimp are pink and opaque, add them to the skillet in a single layer and fry them for two to three minutes on each side.
6. After the shrimp are done, add them to the skillet along with the veggies.
7. Include the cooked brown rice in the skillet along with the veggies and shrimp, and toss to mix.
8. Cover the stir-fry with the low-sodium soy sauce and sesame oil, then mix to cover everything evenly.
9. Cook for a further one to two minutes, or until well cooked.
10. Turn off the heat and, if you'd like, top with sesame seeds and sliced green onions.
11. Enjoy your delicious shrimp stir-fry with brown rice!

7. Caprese Salad with Balsamic Glaze

Ingredients:

- 1 cup cherry tomatoes, halved
- 1 cup fresh mozzarella cheese, cubed
- Fresh basil leaves
- 2 tablespoons extra-virgin olive oil
- 2 tablespoons balsamic glaze
- Salt and pepper to taste

Instructions:

1. Arrange fresh mozzarella cubes and split cherry tomatoes on a serving plate.
2. Place a few fresh basil leaves in between the mozzarella and tomatoes.
3. Distribute the extra-virgin olive oil equally across the mozzarella and tomatoes.
4. To taste, add salt and pepper for seasoning.
5. Drizzle the salad with balsamic glaze to finish.
6. Serve right away to let the flavors mingle.

8. *Lentil Soup with Spinach and Tomatoes*

Ingredients:

- 1 cup dried lentils, rinsed and drained
- 4 cups low-sodium vegetable broth
- 1 onion, diced
- 2 cloves garlic, minced
- 2 carrots, diced
- 2 stalks celery, diced
- 1 can (14.5 oz) diced tomatoes, undrained
- 2 cups fresh spinach leaves, roughly chopped
- 1 teaspoon dried thyme
- 1 teaspoon dried oregano
- Salt and pepper to taste
- 1 tablespoon olive oil

Instructions:

1. Heat the olive oil in a big saucepan or Dutch oven over medium heat.
2. Include the chopped celery, carrots, onion, and garlic in the saucepan. Simmer for 5 to 7 minutes, or until the veggies are tender, stirring periodically.
3. Fill the saucepan with the dry lentils, vegetable broth, chopped tomatoes (including juice), dried oregano, and dried thyme. Mix everything together.

4. After bringing the soup to a boil, turn down the heat. The lentils should be soft after 20 to 25 minutes of simmering under cover.

5. Add the chopped fresh spinach leaves to the cooked lentils. Cook the spinach for a further two to three minutes, or until it wilts.

6. Add salt and pepper to taste when preparing the soup.

7. Before serving, take the pot off of the burner and allow the soup to cool somewhat.

8. Present the heated Lentil Soup with Spinach and Tomatoes, topped with a dollop of Greek yogurt or a sprinkling of grated Parmesan cheese.

9. Turkey and Avocado Lettuce Wraps

Ingredients:

- 1 pound lean ground turkey
- 1 tablespoon olive oil
- 1 small onion, diced
- 2 cloves garlic, minced
- 1 teaspoon ground cumin
- 1 teaspoon chili powder
- 1/2 teaspoon paprika
- Salt and pepper to taste
- 1 large avocado, diced

- Juice of 1 lime
- 1/4 cup chopped fresh cilantro
- 1 head iceberg or butter lettuce, leaves separated

Instructions:

1. In a big pan over medium heat, warm the olive oil.
2. Add the chopped onion to the skillet and simmer for 3–4 minutes, or until it softens.
3. Cook the minced garlic in the pan for another minute, or until it becomes aromatic.
4. Add the ground turkey to the skillet and cook, breaking it up with a spatula, for 5 to 7 minutes, or until it is browned and cooked through.
5. Add the paprika, chili powder, ground cumin, salt, and pepper. Cook for an additional minute to toast the spices.
6. Take the pan off of the burner and thoroughly mix in the chopped cilantro, lime juice, and cubed avocado.
7. To serve, use individual lettuce leaves as wraps and ladle the turkey and avocado mixture onto them.
8. If preferred, garnish with more finely chopped cilantro or lime wedges.
9. Enjoy your turkey and avocado lettuce wraps right away by serving them right away.

10. Sweet Potato and Black Bean Quesadilla

Ingredients:

- 1 medium-sized sweet potato, peeled and diced
- 1 can (15 oz) black beans, drained and rinsed
- 1 cup corn kernels (fresh or frozen)
- 1 teaspoon ground cumin
- 1 teaspoon chili powder
- Salt and pepper to taste
- 4 whole wheat or low-sodium tortillas
- 1 cup shredded low-fat cheese (cheddar or Mexican blend)
- Olive oil or cooking spray for cooking
- Salsa and Greek yogurt for serving (optional)

Instructions:

1. Cook or steam the chopped sweet potato until it becomes soft. Use a fork to gently mash it.
2. Put the black beans, corn, mashed sweet potato, chili powder, ground cumin, salt, and pepper in a bowl. Stir well.
3. Transfer the tortillas to a level surface.
4. Evenly spread the sweet potato and black bean mixture on one half of each tortilla.

5. Top the mixture with the shredded cheese.

6. Using the remaining tortilla, fold it over the contents to form a half-moon.

7. Preheat a skillet over medium heat and give it a quick coat of cooking spray or olive oil.

8. Once the tortilla is brown and the cheese is melted, place the quesadilla in the skillet and cook for two to three minutes on each side.

9. Continue in the same manner with the remaining quesadillas.

10. Cut the cooked quesadillas into wedges.

11. If preferred, present alongside Greek yogurt and salsa.

11. Pasta Primavera with Whole Wheat Pasta

Ingredients:

- 8 oz whole wheat pasta
- 2 tablespoons olive oil
- 3 cloves garlic, minced
- 1 cup broccoli florets
- 1 cup cherry tomatoes, halved
- 1 medium zucchini, sliced
- 1 medium carrot, julienned or thinly sliced
- 1 bell pepper (any color), sliced

- 1/2 cup peas (fresh or frozen)
- 1/4 cup fresh basil, chopped
- 1/4 cup grated Parmesan cheese (optional)
- Salt and pepper to taste
- Red pepper flakes (optional, for heat)

Instructions:

1. Prepare the whole wheat pasta as directed on the packet. After draining, set away.

2. Heat the olive oil in a big skillet over medium heat.

3. Into the skillet add the minced garlic and cook until fragrant.

4. Fill the skillet with the bell pepper, broccoli, cherry tomatoes, zucchini, carrot, and peas. Sauté the veggies for 5 to 7 minutes, or until they are crisp-tender.

5. Add salt, pepper, and, if desired, red pepper flakes to the veggies to season them.

6. Include the cooked whole wheat pasta in the skillet with the veggies and toss to mix.

7. Continue cooking for a further two to three minutes to let the flavors combine.

8. Turn off the heat and add the fresh basil to the skillet.

9. Before serving, you can choose to top the spaghetti with grated Parmesan cheese.

10. Enjoy your kidney-friendly pasta primavera while it's warm!

12. *Grilled Veggie and Hummus Wrap*

Ingredients:

- 1 large whole wheat or spinach tortilla
- 1/4 cup hummus (store-bought or homemade)
- 1/2 cup mixed grilled vegetables (such as bell peppers, zucchini, eggplant, and red onion), sliced
- 1/4 cup crumbled feta cheese (optional)
- Handful of baby spinach leaves
- 1 tablespoon olive oil
- Salt and pepper to taste

Instructions:

1. Turn up the heat to medium-high on an outdoor grill or grill pan.
2. Evenly coat the sliced mixed veggies with a mixture of olive oil, salt, and pepper.
3. Grill the veggies until they are soft and have grill marks, 3 to 4 minutes on each side.
4. Place the tortilla in a level, spotless manner.

5. Evenly cover the tortilla with hummus, leaving a thin border all the way around.

6. Evenly distribute the grilled veggies on top of the hummus.

7. Top the veggies with the crumbled feta cheese, if using.

8. Add a few young spinach leaves on top.

9. To create a wrap, fold in the tortilla's sides and then tightly roll it up from the bottom.

10. If preferred, cut the wrap in half diagonally, and serve right away.

13. Baked Cod with Lemon and Herbs

Ingredients:

- 4 cod filets (about 6 ounces each)
- 2 tablespoons olive oil
- 2 cloves garlic, minced
- Zest of 1 lemon
- Juice of 1 lemon
- 1 tablespoon chopped fresh parsley
- 1 tablespoon chopped fresh dill
- Salt and pepper to taste
- Lemon slices for garnish

Instructions:

1. Set the oven temperature to 375°F, or 190°C. Apply cooking spray or olive oil sparingly to a baking dish.
2. Arrange the cod filets, with a small space between each, in the baking dish that has been prepared.
3. Combine the olive oil, minced garlic, zest and juice of the lemon, chopped parsley, and chopped dill in a small bowl.
4. Make sure the cod filets are uniformly covered by drizzling them with the lemon and herb mixture.
5. Toss in some salt and pepper to taste and season the cod filets.
6. For added taste, garnish each fish filet with a slice of lemon.
7. Bake the cod filets for 12 to 15 minutes, or until the cod flakes easily with a fork and is cooked through.
8. After cooking, take the cod filets out of the oven and give them a few minutes to rest before serving.
9. Garnish the hot baked cod with lemon and herbs with more fresh herbs, if you'd like.

14. Quinoa and Roasted Vegetable Stuffed Peppers

Ingredients:

- 4 large bell peppers, halved and seeds removed
- 1 cup quinoa, rinsed
- 2 cups low-sodium vegetable broth or water
- 2 tablespoons olive oil
- 1 small eggplant, diced
- 1 zucchini, diced
- 1 red onion, diced
- 1 red bell pepper, diced
- 2 cloves garlic, minced
- 1 teaspoon dried oregano
- 1 teaspoon dried thyme
- Salt and pepper to taste
- 1/2 cup crumbled feta cheese (optional)
- Fresh parsley for garnish

Instructions:

1. Set the oven's temperature to 400°F, or 200°C.
2. Transfer the split bell peppers to a baking tray and keep them out of the way.
3. Bring water or vegetable broth to a boil in a saucepan. After adding the quinoa, lower the heat, cover, and simmer until the quinoa is cooked and the liquid has been absorbed—about 15 minutes. Using a fork, fluff and set aside.
4. Heat the olive oil in a big pan over medium heat.

5. Fill the skillet with diced eggplant, zucchini, red onion, red bell pepper, and minced garlic. Until the veggies are soft, sauté them.

6. Add salt, pepper, dried thyme, and oregano.

7. Mix the cooked quinoa with the sautéed veggies. Add some crumbled feta cheese if desired.

8. Place the quinoa and roasted veggie mixture into each half of a bell pepper.

9. Bake the baking dish in the preheated oven for 20 to 25 minutes, or until the peppers are soft, covered with foil.

10. Before serving, garnish with fresh parsley.

15. Chicken and Vegetable Skewers with Greek Yogurt Dip

Ingredients:

For the Chicken and Vegetable Skewers:

- 1 pound boneless, skinless chicken breasts, cut into cubes
- 2 bell peppers, cut into chunks
- 1 red onion, cut into chunks
- 1 zucchini, sliced into rounds
- 8-10 wooden or metal skewers
- 2 tablespoons olive oil

- 2 cloves garlic, minced
- 1 teaspoon dried oregano
- 1 teaspoon dried thyme
- Salt and pepper to taste

For the Greek Yogurt Dip:

- 1 cup plain Greek yogurt (low-fat or non-fat)
- 1 tablespoon lemon juice
- 1 tablespoon chopped fresh dill
- 1 clove garlic, minced
- Salt and pepper to taste

Instructions:

1. To keep wooden skewers from burning on the grill, immerse them in water for at least half an hour.
2. Combine the olive oil, salt, pepper, dried thyme, dried oregano, and chopped garlic in a bowl.
3. Alternating between the chicken and the veggies, thread the chicken cubes and the prepped vegetables onto the skewers.
4. Evenly coat the skewers by brushing them with the olive oil mixture.
5. Turn the heat up to medium-high on a grill or grill pan.
6. Grill the skewers for 8 to 10 minutes, rotating them halfway through, or until the veggies are soft

and have a hint of sea and the chicken is cooked through.

7. Make the Greek yogurt dip while the skewers are cooking. Combine the Greek yogurt, lemon juice, minced garlic, chopped fresh dill, salt, and pepper in a small bowl.

8. Present the freshly grilled Chicken and Vegetable Skewers beside a side serving of Greek yogurt dip for dipping.

Healthy and Delicious Dinner Recipes For Seniors

1. Baked Herb-Crusted Salmon with Asparagus

Ingredients:

- 4 salmon filets (about 6 ounces each)
- 1 bunch asparagus, woody ends trimmed
- 2 tablespoons olive oil
- 2 cloves garlic, minced
- Zest of 1 lemon
- Juice of 1 lemon

- 1 tablespoon chopped fresh parsley
- 1 tablespoon chopped fresh dill
- 1 tablespoon chopped fresh thyme
- Salt and pepper to taste
- Lemon slices for garnish

Instructions:

Set the oven temperature to 400°F, or 200°C. Cover a baking sheet with foil or parchment paper.

2. Arrange the salmon filets, allowing space between each one, on half of the baking sheet that has been prepared.

3. Make sure the asparagus spears are arranged in a single layer on the opposite side of the baking sheet.

4. Combine the olive oil, minced garlic, zest and juice of the lemon, chopped parsley, chopped dill, and chopped thyme in a small bowl.

5. Use your hands or a brush to evenly cover the salmon filets and asparagus after drizzling them with the herb mixture.

6. Add salt and pepper to taste and season the asparagus and salmon filets.

7. For added taste, place slices of lemon over the salmon filets.

8. Bake for 12 to 15 minutes in a preheated oven, or until the asparagus is crisp-tender and the salmon is cooked through and flakes readily with a fork.

9. After the salmon and asparagus are done, take the baking sheet out of the oven and allow them to rest for a few minutes before serving.

10. Garnish the baked herb-crusted salmon with lemon slices or more fresh herbs, if you'd like, and serve it hot with asparagus.

2. Vegetable Stir-Fry with Tofu and Brown Rice

Ingredients:

- 1 block (14-16 ounces) firm tofu, pressed and cubed
- 2 cups cooked brown rice
- 2 tablespoons soy sauce (low-sodium if preferred)
- 1 tablespoon sesame oil
- 2 tablespoons vegetable oil, divided
- 2 cloves garlic, minced
- 1 tablespoon minced ginger
- 1 small onion, thinly sliced
- 2 cups mixed vegetables (such as bell peppers, broccoli, snap peas, carrots), chopped
- 1 cup sliced mushrooms
- Salt and pepper to taste
- **Optional garnish**: chopped green onions, sesame seeds

Instructions:

1. Heat one tablespoon of vegetable oil in a big pan or wok over medium heat.
2. Add the cubed tofu to the skillet and cook for 5 to 7 minutes, or until golden brown on both sides. After taking the tofu out of the skillet, set it aside.
3. Add the last tablespoon of vegetable oil to the same skillet.
4. Add the finely chopped ginger and garlic to the pan and heat for approximately one minute, or until aromatic.
5. Add the sliced onion to the skillet and simmer for three to four minutes, or until softened.
6. Cook for a further five to seven minutes, or until the veggies are crisp-tender, after stirring in the mixed vegetables and sliced mushrooms.
7. Add the cooked brown rice to the skillet along with the tofu that has been cooked.
8. Pour the rice, veggies, and tofu with the soy sauce and sesame oil, then combine everything until it's well covered.
9. To taste, add salt and pepper for seasoning.
10. Cook, stirring periodically, for a further two to three minutes, or until everything is well cooked.
11. Take off the heat and, if you'd like, top with chopped green onions and sesame seeds.

12. Plate the hot vegetable stir-fry with brown rice and tofu, and savor!

3. Cauliflower and Chickpea Curry

Ingredients:

- 1 medium-sized cauliflower, cut into florets
- 1 can (15 oz) chickpeas, drained and rinsed
- 1 large onion, finely chopped
- 3 cloves garlic, minced
- 1 tablespoon ginger, grated
- 2 tablespoons vegetable oil
- 1 can (14 oz) diced tomatoes
- 1 can (14 oz) coconut milk
- 1 tablespoon tomato paste
- 2 teaspoons curry powder
- 1 teaspoon ground cumin
- 1 teaspoon ground coriander
- 1/2 teaspoon turmeric
- 1/2 teaspoon chili powder (adjust to taste)
- Salt and pepper to taste
- Fresh cilantro for garnish
- Cooked rice or naan for serving

Instructions:

1. To begin, rinse the chickpeas well and chop the cauliflower into bite-sized florets.

2. Heat vegetable oil in a big pot or deep pan over medium heat. Add the chopped onion and cook it until it softens and turns transparent.

3. Add the grated ginger and minced garlic, and simmer for one more minute, or until the kitchen smells delicious.

4. Add the turmeric, chili powder, curry powder, powdered cumin, ground coriander, salt, and pepper. To enhance the flavors, cook, stirring constantly, for one to two minutes.

5. Fill the saucepan with chopped tomatoes and tomato paste. Cook, stirring constantly, for 5 to 7 minutes, or until the tomatoes start to break down.

6. Fill the saucepan with the drained chickpeas and cauliflower florets. Stir to coat in the aromatic mixture of spices and tomatoes.

7. Add the coconut milk, mix, and simmer the curry for a few minutes. Once the cauliflower is soft, reduce the heat and simmer it for 15 to 20 minutes.

8. After tasting the curry, taste and adjust the spices and salt to your taste.

9. You can also serve the cauliflower and chickpea curry over naan bread or over cooked rice. Add fresh cilantro as a garnish.

4. Turkey and Quinoa Stuffed Bell Peppers

Ingredients:

- 4 large bell peppers, halved and seeds removed
- 1 cup quinoa, rinsed
- 2 cups low-sodium chicken or vegetable broth
- 1 tablespoon olive oil
- 1 onion, finely chopped
- 2 cloves garlic, minced
- 1 pound ground turkey
- 1 can (14 oz) diced tomatoes, drained
- 1 teaspoon ground cumin
- 1 teaspoon smoked paprika
- Salt and pepper to taste
- 1 cup black beans, drained and rinsed
- 1 cup corn kernels (fresh or frozen)
- 1 cup shredded cheese (cheddar or Mexican blend)
- Fresh cilantro for garnish (optional)

Instructions:

1. Start by getting the quinoa ready. After washing one cup of quinoa, simmer it in two cups of vegetable or low-sodium chicken broth. Cook the quinoa and absorb the liquid by simmering it. Put it away.

2. Set the oven temperature to 375°F, or 190°C. Make sure to remove the seeds and membranes by cutting four big bell peppers in half lengthwise.

3. Heat one tablespoon of olive oil in a big pan over medium heat. Finely chop an onion and sauté it until it becomes tender. To unleash the flavors, add two cloves of minced garlic and simmer for a further minute.

4. Add 1 pound of the ground turkey to the skillet, crumble it using a spoon, and heat it until it's deliciously browned. One teaspoon each of ground cumin, smoked paprika, salt, and pepper are used to season the turkey. Add a can of drained chopped tomatoes and simmer, stirring, for a few minutes, until the flavors meld well.

5. Put the cooked quinoa, one cup of rinsed and drained black beans, one cup of frozen or fresh corn, and the spiced turkey mixture in a big mixing bowl. Make sure the ingredients are thoroughly combined.

6. Transfer the bell pepper halves to a baking tray and stuff the turkey and quinoa mixture into each half to a considerable degree. Sprinkle some shredded cheese (you may use cheddar or a Mexican mix for extra taste) on top of each filled pepper.

7. Bake the baking dish in the preheated oven for about 25 to 30 minutes, or until the peppers are soft, covered with foil.

8. Before serving, top the filled peppers with fresh cilantro if you'd like.

5. Zucchini Noodles with Pesto and Cherry Tomatoes

Ingredients:

- 4 medium-sized zucchinis, spiralized into noodles
- 1 cup cherry tomatoes, halved
- 1/2 cup homemade or store-bought pesto sauce
- 2 tablespoons olive oil
- Salt and pepper to taste
- Grated Parmesan cheese for garnish (optional)
- Fresh basil leaves for garnish

Instructions:

1. Using a spiralizer or vegetable peeler, spiralize the zucchini into noodles.
2. Heat the olive oil in a big skillet over medium heat.
3. Add the zucchini noodles to the skillet and cook them for two to three minutes, or until they are slightly crunchy but still soft.

4. Add the cherry tomatoes and continue to sauté for a further one to two minutes, or until the tomatoes are well heated.

5. Add the pesto sauce to the pan and mix the tomatoes and zucchini noodles until they are covered evenly.

6. To taste, add salt and pepper for seasoning. Keep in mind that salt is a common ingredient in pesto.

7. Turn off the heat and place the noodles on serving dishes.

8. For an explosion of flavor, garnish with fresh basil leaves and grated Parmesan cheese, if preferred.

9. Serve right away and savor your tasty and light zucchini noodles with cherry tomatoes and pesto!

6. Grilled Chicken with Lemon-Herb Marinade

Ingredients:

- 4 boneless, skinless chicken breasts
- 1/4 cup olive oil
- Zest and juice of 1 lemon
- 2 cloves garlic, minced
- 1 tablespoon chopped fresh parsley

- 1 tablespoon chopped fresh thyme
- 1 tablespoon chopped fresh rosemary
- Salt and pepper to taste
- Lemon wedges for serving

Instructions:

1. To create the marinade, combine the olive oil, lemon zest, lemon juice, minced garlic, chopped parsley, chopped thyme, and chopped rosemary in a small bowl.

2. Put the chicken breasts in a plastic bag that can be sealed or in a shallow plate.

3. Cover the chicken with the marinade, being careful to coat each breast equally. To let the flavors combine and the chicken marinade, cover the dish or seal the bag and place it in the refrigerator for at least 30 minutes or up to 4 hours.

4. Turn the heat up to medium-high on your grill.

5. Take the chicken out of the marinade, shake off any extra, and throw away any marinade that is left.

6. Toss in more salt and pepper to taste and season the chicken breasts.

7. Grill the chicken breasts for 6 to 8 minutes on each side, or until the outside has grill marks and the chicken is cooked through and no longer pink in the middle.

8. When the chicken breasts are done, take them from the grill and give them a few minutes to rest before serving.

9. Present the hot Grilled Chicken with Lemon-Herb Marinade, accompanied by lemon wedges for the chicken to be squeezed over.

7. Eggplant Parmesan with Whole Wheat Pasta

Ingredients:

- 1 large eggplant, sliced into 1/2-inch rounds
- 1 cup whole wheat breadcrumbs
- 2 eggs, beaten
- 2 cups marinara sauce
- 1 cup shredded mozzarella cheese
- 1/2 cup grated Parmesan cheese
- 1 teaspoon dried oregano
- 1 teaspoon dried basil
- Salt and pepper to taste
- 2 tablespoons olive oil
- 8 oz whole wheat pasta, cooked according to package instructions
- Fresh basil leaves for garnish

Instructions:

1. Turn the oven on to 375°F, or 190°C.

2. Combine whole wheat breadcrumbs, salt, pepper, dried oregano, and dried basil in a small basin.

3. Gently press the breadcrumb mixture over the eggplant slices after dipping them into the beaten eggs and making sure they are well covered.

4. Heat the olive oil in a big pan over medium heat. Cook the breaded eggplant slices until golden brown, 2 to 3 minutes each side. After cooking, transfer the slices to a paper towel to drain excess oil.

5. Apply a thin layer of marinara sauce to a baking dish. Arrange the cooked eggplant slices in a single layer on top.

6. Top the eggplant layer with grated Parmesan cheese and shredded mozzarella. Continue layering the ingredients until all are utilized, and then top with a layer of cheese.

7. Bake for 25 to 30 minutes, or until the cheese is bubbling and melted, in a preheated oven.

8. Prepare whole wheat pasta per package directions while the eggplant parmesan bakes.

9. Top whole wheat pasta with the eggplant parmesan.

10. For a splash of freshness, garnish with fresh basil leaves.

11. Savor your tasty and healthful Whole Wheat Pasta with Eggplant Parmesan!

8. Spinach and Feta Stuffed Chicken Breast

Ingredients:

- 4 boneless, skinless chicken breasts
- 2 cups fresh spinach leaves, chopped
- 1/2 cup crumbled feta cheese
- 2 cloves garlic, minced
- 1 tablespoon olive oil
- 1 teaspoon dried oregano
- Salt and pepper to taste
- Toothpicks or kitchen twine

Instructions:

1. Set the oven temperature to 375°F, or 190°C.
2. Heat the olive oil in a skillet over medium heat. Once aromatic, sauté the minced garlic for one minute.
3. Add the chopped spinach to the skillet and heat it for two to three minutes, or until it wilts.
4. Take the pan off of the burner and thoroughly mix in the feta cheese crumbles. Let the mixture cool down a little.

5. To provide a pocket for the filling, butterfly the chicken breasts by cutting a horizontal incision across the middle, taking cautious not to cut all the way through, while the spinach and feta mixture cools.

6. Sprinkle salt, pepper, and dry oregano into each chicken breast.

7. Tighten the opening of each chicken breast with toothpicks or kitchen twine after stuffing it with a piece of the spinach and feta mixture.

8. With the seam side down, put the packed chicken breasts in a baking dish.

9. Bake for 25 to 30 minutes, or until the chicken is well cooked and the middle is no longer pink, in a preheated oven.

10. Before serving, take out the kitchen twine or toothpicks.

11. Present the heated chicken breast stuffed with spinach and feta, and savor!

9. Lentil and Vegetable Stew

Ingredients:

- 1 cup dry green or brown lentils, rinsed and drained
- 1 onion, finely chopped

- 2 carrots, peeled and diced
- 2 celery stalks, diced
- 3 cloves garlic, minced
- 1 can (14 oz) diced tomatoes
- 6 cups vegetable broth
- 1 teaspoon ground cumin
- 1 teaspoon ground coriander
- 1/2 teaspoon smoked paprika
- 1 bay leaf
- Salt and pepper to taste
- 2 cups chopped kale or spinach
- 2 tablespoons olive oil
- Fresh parsley for garnish

Instructions:

1. Heat the olive oil in a big saucepan over medium heat. Add the chopped celery, carrots, and onion. Sauté the veggies till they get tender.
2. Add the minced garlic and cook it for a minute more, or until it becomes aromatic.
3. Add the chopped tomatoes, dried lentils, smoked paprika, bay leaf, vegetable broth, ground cumin, and ground coriander. Season with salt and pepper. Mix well to blend.
4. After bringing the stew to a boil, lower the heat to a simmer, cover it, and let it cook for 25 to 30 minutes, or until the lentils are soft.

5. Stir the chopped spinach or kale into the saucepan until it wilts.

6. Taste and, if necessary, adjust seasoning.

7. Before serving, take out the bay leaf.

8. Spoon the vegetable and lentil stew into individual dishes.

9. Add some fresh parsley as a garnish for a taste and color pop.

10. Present and savor this filling and nutritious lentil and vegetable stew!

10. Mushroom and Spinach Quiche with Whole Grain Crust

Ingredients:

For the Whole Grain Crust:

- 1 1/2 cups whole wheat flour
- 1/2 cup rolled oats
- 1/2 teaspoon salt
- 1/2 cup cold unsalted butter, cut into small cubes
- 4-6 tablespoons ice water

For the Mushroom and Spinach Filling:

- 1 tablespoon olive oil
- 1 small onion, diced
- 2 cloves garlic, minced
- 8 ounces mushrooms, sliced
- 2 cups fresh spinach leaves, chopped
- Salt and pepper to taste
- 4 large eggs
- 1 cup milk (any kind you prefer)
- 1/2 cup shredded cheese (such as Gruyere, Swiss, or cheddar)

Instructions:

For the Whole Grain Crust:

1. Place the rolled oats, whole wheat flour, and salt in a large basin.
2. Combine the flour mixture with the chilled cubed butter.
3. Until the mixture resembles coarse crumbs, knead the butter into the flour with your fingertips or a pastry cutter.
4. One spoonful at a time, gradually add the ice water and stir until the dough comes together. Maybe you won't use all of the water.
5. Press the dough into a disk, cover with plastic wrap, and chill for at least half an hour.

For the Mushroom and Spinach Filling:

1. Set the oven temperature to 375°F, or 190°C.

2. Heat the olive oil in a big skillet over medium heat. Add the chopped garlic and onion, and simmer for 3–4 minutes, or until the ingredients are softened.

3. Add the sliced mushrooms to the skillet and simmer for 5 to 7 minutes, or until they release their moisture and get soft.

4. Add the chopped spinach and simmer for two to three minutes, or until wilted. To taste, add salt and pepper for seasoning. Take off the heat and place aside.

5. Beat the eggs and milk together thoroughly in another basin. Add pepper and salt for seasoning.

6. Using a surface dusted with flour, roll out the cold dough into a circle that fits into a 9-inch pie plate.

7. Carefully move the rolled-out dough to the pie plate, pressing it into the edges and bottom.

8. Evenly distribute the combination of spinach and mushrooms over the crust.

9. Cover the spinach and mushroom combination with the egg and milk mixture.

10. Top with cheese that has been shredded.

11. Bake for 30 to 35 minutes, or until the crust is golden brown and the quiche has set, in a preheated oven.

12. Before slicing and serving, let the quiche cool for a few minutes.

11. Baked Cod with Mediterranean Salsa

Ingredients:

- 4 cod filets (about 6 oz each)
- 2 tablespoons olive oil
- 1 teaspoon dried oregano
- 1 teaspoon dried thyme
- 1 teaspoon paprika
- Salt and pepper to taste
- 1 cup cherry tomatoes, halved
- 1/2 cucumber, diced
- 1/4 cup Kalamata olives, sliced
- 1/4 cup red onion, finely chopped
- 2 tablespoons feta cheese, crumbled
- 1 tablespoon fresh lemon juice
- Fresh parsley for garnish

Instructions:

1. Set the oven's temperature to 400°F, or 200°C.
2. Arrange the cod filets on a baking sheet that has been gently oiled or covered with parchment paper.

3. Combine olive oil, paprika, dried thyme, dried oregano, salt, and pepper in a small bowl. Drizzle the blend onto the cod filets.

4. Bake for 15 to 20 minutes in a preheated oven, or until the cod is well cooked and flakes readily with a fork.

5. Make the Mediterranean salsa while the cod bakes. Combine cherry tomatoes, feta cheese, red onion, chopped cucumber, Kalamata olives, and fresh lemon juice in a bowl. Gently toss to combine.

6. After the cod is cooked, take it out of the oven and top it with a spoonful of Mediterranean salsa.

7. Add some fresh parsley as a garnish for a pop of color and freshness.

8. Serve your preferred side dishes with the Baked Cod and Mediterranean Salsa.

9. Savor this tasty and refreshing meal with a Mediterranean flair!

12. Vegetarian Chili with Kidney Beans

Ingredients:

- 2 tablespoons olive oil
- 1 large onion, diced
- 2 bell peppers (any color), diced

- 2 cloves garlic, minced
- 2 carrots, diced
- 2 celery stalks, diced
- 1 jalapeño pepper, seeded and diced (optional, for added heat)
- 1 tablespoon chili powder
- 1 teaspoon ground cumin
- 1 teaspoon smoked paprika
- 1 teaspoon dried oregano
- 1/2 teaspoon ground cinnamon
- 1 can (14 oz) diced tomatoes, undrained
- 2 cans (15 oz each) kidney beans, drained and rinsed
- 2 cups vegetable broth
- Salt and pepper to taste
- **Optional toppings:** chopped fresh cilantro, sliced green onions, shredded cheese, sour cream, avocado slices

Instructions:

1. In a big saucepan or Dutch oven, warm the olive oil over medium heat.
2. Include in the saucepan the chopped onion, bell peppers, garlic, carrots, celery, and jalapeño pepper (if using). Cook for 8 to 10 minutes, stirring often, or until the veggies are tender.
3. Add the ground cinnamon, dried oregano, smoked paprika, ground cumin, and chili powder.

Cook until the spices become aromatic, about one more minute.

4. Fill the saucepan with the kidney beans that have been washed and drained, chopped tomatoes together with their liquids, and vegetable broth. Mix everything together.

5. Simmer the chili for a short while before turning down the heat. For the chili to thicken and the flavors to combine, cover and cook gently for 20 to 25 minutes, stirring from time to time.

6. Check for seasoning by tasting and adding salt and pepper as required.

7. Top the hot vegetarian chili with kidney beans with your preferred toppings, such as avocado slices, shredded cheese, sour cream, chopped fresh cilantro, or sliced green onions.

13. Pesto Zoodle Bowl with Grilled Shrimp

Ingredients:

- 1 pound large shrimp, peeled and deveined
- 2 tablespoons olive oil
- Salt and pepper to taste
- 4 medium zucchinis, spiralized into noodles
- 1/2 cup cherry tomatoes, halved

- 1/4 cup pine nuts, toasted
- 1/2 cup freshly grated Parmesan cheese
- 1/2 cup homemade or store-bought pesto sauce
- Fresh basil leaves for garnish
- Lemon wedges for serving

Instructions:

1. Turn the heat up to medium-high on the grill or grill pan.
2. Combine salt, pepper, and olive oil in a bowl with the peeled and deveined shrimp.
3. Grill the shrimp for two to three minutes on each side, or until they are fully cooked and opaque. Put aside.
4. Heat a tiny quantity of olive oil in a big skillet over medium heat. When the zucchini noodles are just cooked, add them and sauté for two to three minutes.
5. Spoon the noodles made from zucchini into serving dishes.
6. Arrange grilled shrimp, cherry tomatoes, and toasted pine nuts on top of the zoodles.
7. Pour pesto sauce into the bowl, making sure it coats everything evenly.
8. Top with freshly shredded Parmesan cheese.
9. Add some fresh basil leaves as a garnish for a taste explosion.

10. Present the Pesto Zoodle Bowl with Grilled Shrimp right away, adding some zest with lemon wedges.

11. Savor the abundance of tastes and textures in this bright, airy meal!

14. Baked Teriyaki Chicken with Broccoli

Ingredients:

For the Teriyaki Chicken:

- 4 boneless, skinless chicken breasts
- 1/2 cup soy sauce (low-sodium if preferred)
- 1/4 cup honey
- 2 tablespoons rice vinegar
- 2 cloves garlic, minced
- 1 teaspoon grated ginger
- 1 tablespoon cornstarch (optional, for thickening)

For the Broccoli:

- 2 heads of broccoli, cut into florets
- 2 tablespoons olive oil
- Salt and pepper to taste

Optional Garnish:

- Sesame seeds
- Sliced green onions

Instructions:

Set the oven temperature to 400°F, or 200°C. For easier cleanup, line a baking sheet with foil or parchment paper.

2. Over medium heat, mix the soy sauce, honey, rice vinegar, grated ginger, and chopped garlic in a small saucepan. Simmer and cook the mixture for two to three minutes.

3. Make a slurry out of the cornstarch and two tablespoons of water if you would like your sauce to be thicker. After adding the slurry to the sauce, heat it for a further one to two minutes, or until it slightly thickens. Take off the heat and place aside.

4. Transfer the chicken breasts to the baking sheet that has been ready. Transfer half of the teriyaki sauce to the chicken and set aside the remaining half for another time.

5. Bake the chicken for 20 to 25 minutes, or until it's cooked through and the middle is no longer pink, in a preheated oven.

6. Toss the broccoli florets with olive oil, salt, and pepper on a separate baking sheet while the chicken bakes.

7. Put the broccoli in the oven in a single layer and roast it for 15 to 20 minutes, or until it is soft and has a faint browning around the edges.

8. Take the chicken and broccoli out of the oven when they're done.

9. Cover the roasted chicken with the leftover teriyaki sauce.

10. If wanted, top the hot baked teriyaki chicken with broccoli with sliced green onions and sesame seeds.

15. Cabbage and Turkey Sauté with Brown Rice

Ingredients:

- 1 pound ground turkey
- 2 tablespoons olive oil
- 1 onion, finely chopped
- 2 cloves garlic, minced
- 4 cups green cabbage, shredded
- 1 carrot, julienned
- 1 bell pepper, thinly sliced
- 2 cups cooked brown rice
- 2 tablespoons low-sodium soy sauce
- 1 tablespoon hoisin sauce
- 1 teaspoon sesame oil

- Salt and pepper to taste
- Green onions for garnish
- Sesame seeds for garnish

Instructions:

1. Heat the olive oil in a big pan or wok over medium-high heat.
2. Add the ground turkey to the skillet and use a spoon to break it up while it cooks until browned.
3. Give the turkey some minced garlic and onion. The onion should be mellow and fragrant after sautéing.
4. Add the sliced bell pepper, julienned carrot, and shredded cabbage. Cook the veggies for five to seven minutes, or until they are crisp-tender.
5. Include the cooked brown rice in the skillet along with the veggies and turkey.
6. Combine the sesame oil, hoisin sauce, and low-sodium soy sauce in a small bowl. Cover the turkey and vegetable combination with the sauce.
7. To taste, add salt and pepper for seasoning. Mix everything until well incorporated.
8. Cook the dish for a further two to three minutes, or until it is well cooked and the flavors have blended.
9. Add chopped green onions and sesame seeds to the brown rice and cabbage sauté.

10. Enjoy this tasty and filling sauté over brown rice right away by serving it immediately!

Easy Snacks and Sides For Seniors

1. Greek Yogurt with Fresh Berries

Ingredients:

- 1 cup Greek yogurt
- 1/2 cup strawberries, hulled and sliced
- 1/2 cup blueberries
- 1/2 cup raspberries
- 1 tablespoon honey
- 1/4 cup granola (optional)
- Mint leaves for garnish

Instructions:

1. Measure out one cup of Greek yogurt into a serving dish.
2. Top the yogurt with cut raspberries, blueberries, and strawberries.
3. Drizzle yogurt and fresh berries with honey.
4. You may add extra crunch by scattering granola on top if you'd like.
5. Add some mint leaves as a garnish for a refreshing touch.
6. Present the Greek yogurt with fresh berries right away, then have this tasty and nourishing treat!

2. Hummus and Veggie Sticks

Ingredients:

- 1 cup hummus (store-bought or homemade)
- **Assorted vegetables for dipping, such as:**
  - Carrot sticks
  - Celery sticks
  - Cucumber slices
  - Bell pepper strips
  - Cherry tomatoes
  - Snap peas
  - Radish slices
  - Broccoli florets
  - Cauliflower florets

Instructions:

1. Spoon the store-bought hummus into a serving dish if using it. If you're creating your own hummus, follow your preferred recipe and pour the mixture into a serving bowl.
2. Wash and chop the various veggies into sticks, slices, or florets in preparation for dipping.
3. On a serving tray or dish, arrange the prepped veggies around the hummus bowl.
4. Present the veggie sticks and hummus right away, and savor!

3. Cucumber and Tomato Salad with Feta

Ingredients:

- 2 cucumbers, thinly sliced
- 2 cups cherry tomatoes, halved
- 1/2 red onion, thinly sliced
- 1/2 cup crumbled feta cheese
- 1/4 cup Kalamata olives, sliced
- 2 tablespoons extra-virgin olive oil
- 1 tablespoon red wine vinegar
- 1 teaspoon dried oregano
- Salt and pepper to taste
- Fresh parsley for garnish

Instructions:

1. Combine thinly sliced red onion, cucumbers, and cherry tomatoes in half in a big bowl.
2. Fill the bowl with feta cheese crumbles and chopped Kalamata olives.
3. Combine the extra-virgin olive oil, red wine vinegar, dried oregano, salt, and pepper in a small bowl.
4. Pour the dressing over the combination of feta, tomato, and cucumber.
5. Gently toss the salad until every component is well covered.
6. Add some fresh parsley as a garnish for taste and color.

7. Present the Cucumber and Tomato Salad with Feta either as a light and delicious salad on its own or as a pleasant side dish.

8. Savor this colorful, tasty, and easy salad!

4. Baked Sweet Potato Fries

Ingredients:

- 2 large sweet potatoes
- 2 tablespoons olive oil
- 1 teaspoon paprika
- 1/2 teaspoon garlic powder
- 1/2 teaspoon onion powder
- 1/2 teaspoon salt
- 1/4 teaspoon black pepper
- **Optional:** chopped fresh parsley or cilantro for garnish

Instructions:

1. Set the oven's temperature to 425°F (220°C). For easier cleanup, line a baking pan with aluminum foil or parchment paper.

2. Give the sweet potatoes a good wash and scrape. Although keeping the skin on provides more fiber and nutrients, you may peel them if you'd like.

3. Slice the sweet potatoes into fries or wedges of the same size. To guarantee even cooking, try to make them as uniform as you can.

4. Place the sweet potato fries in a big basin and toss them to cover them equally with a mixture of olive oil, paprika, onion, garlic, and black pepper.

5. Spread out, but do not crowd, the seasoned sweet potato fries in a single layer on the baking sheet. This will aid in their beautiful crisping.

6. Bake the fries for 20 to 25 minutes in a preheated oven, turning them over halfway through, or until the exterior is crispy and golden brown and the interior is soft.

7. After cooking, take the sweet potato fries out of the oven and give them a little time to cool.

8. If preferred, garnish with finely chopped fresh parsley or cilantro, and serve hot.

5. Apple Slices with Almond Butter

Ingredients:

- 2 apples, cored and sliced
- 1/4 cup almond butter
- 1 tablespoon honey (optional)
- 1/2 teaspoon cinnamon (optional)
- Sliced almonds for garnish (optional)

Instructions:

1. Cut two apples into small wedges after coreing them.

2. Heat the almond butter in a small bowl for a few seconds in the microwave, just long enough to make it spreadable.

3. Put the apple slices in a platter or dish arrangement.

4. Drizzle the apple slices with almond butter.

5. For an extra delicious touch, you can optionally sprinkle honey over the almond butter.

6. To add even more flavor, sprinkle cinnamon on top.

7. For an extra crunch, garnish with chopped almonds.

8. Present the Almond Butter-Topping Apple Slices as a wholesome and filling snack.

9. Savor the delicious contrast of creamy almond butter and sweet, crisp apples!

6. Whole Grain Crackers with Cheese

Ingredients:

- Whole grain crackers (store-bought or homemade)

- **Assorted cheeses, such as:**
- Cheddar
- Swiss
- Gouda
- Pepper Jack
- Brie
- Goat cheese
- **Optional toppings:**
- Sliced fruits (apples, pears, grapes)
- Nuts (walnuts, almonds, pecans)
- Honey or jam

Instructions:

1. Place the whole grain crackers onto a board or dish for serving.
2. Cut the various cheeses into slices or cubes and place them on the dish next to the crackers.
3. Place any optional toppings on the dish, either next to the cheese or on top of it, if you're using them.
4. Present the Whole Grain Crackers and Cheese right away, then savor!

7. Roasted Chickpeas with Herbs

Ingredients:

- 2 cans (15 oz each) chickpeas, drained and rinsed
- 2 tablespoons olive oil
- 1 teaspoon dried thyme
- 1 teaspoon dried rosemary
- 1 teaspoon ground cumin
- 1/2 teaspoon garlic powder
- 1/2 teaspoon onion powder
- 1/2 teaspoon paprika
- Salt and pepper to taste

Instructions:

1. Set the oven's temperature to 400°F, or 200°C.
2. After giving the chickpeas a good rinse and draining, blot them dry with paper towels.
3. Combine the chickpeas with olive oil, paprika, onion, garlic, dried thyme, dried rosemary, ground cumin, and salt and pepper in a bowl. Take care to coat the chickpeas evenly.
4. Arrange the seasoned chickpeas in a single layer on a baking pan.
5. Roast the chickpeas for 25 to 30 minutes in a preheated oven, shaking the pan halfway through to ensure equal roasting, or until they are golden brown and crispy.
6. Take them out of the oven and give them some time to cool.

7. Present the Herbed Roasted Chickpeas as a crispy and savory snack.
8. Savor these roasted chickpeas with herb infusion as a filling and healthy snack!

8. Guacamole with Baked Tortilla Chips

Ingredients:

For the Guacamole:

- 2 ripe avocados
- 1 small onion, finely diced
- 1 tomato, diced
- 1 jalapeño pepper, seeded and minced
- 2 cloves garlic, minced
- Juice of 1 lime
- 2 tablespoons chopped fresh cilantro
- Salt and pepper to taste

For the Baked Tortilla Chips:

- 6 corn tortillas
- Cooking spray or olive oil
- Salt to taste

Instructions:

For the Guacamole:

1. Scoop the avocado flesh into a mixing bowl after cutting the avocados in half and removing the pits.
2. Using a fork, mash the avocado until the appropriate consistency is achieved (some people like it chunky, while others want it smooth).
3. To the mashed avocado, add the finely chopped onion, diced tomato, minced garlic, minced jalapeño pepper, lime juice, chopped cilantro, salt, and pepper. Mix thoroughly.
4. Taste and adjust the seasoning, adding extra lime juice, salt, or pepper to taste.
5. To let the flavors combine, cover the guacamole and chill it for at least 30 minutes.

For the Baked Tortilla Chips:

1. Set the oven temperature to 175°C, or 350°F.
2. Stack the corn tortillas and use a sharp knife or pizza cutter to cut them into wedges or strips.
3. Place the tortilla strips or wedges in a single layer on a parchment paper-lined baking sheet.
4. Lightly brush or spray the tortilla wedges or strips with olive oil or cooking spray.
5. Toss in a little salt over the tortilla strips or wedges.

6. Bake, rotating them midway through for even baking, in a preheated oven for 10 to 12 minutes, or until golden brown and crispy.

7. Before serving, take the cooked tortilla chips out of the oven and allow them to cool somewhat.

9. Caprese Skewers with Cherry Tomatoes and Mozzarella

Ingredients:

- 1 pint cherry tomatoes
- 1 package (8 oz) fresh mozzarella balls
- Fresh basil leaves
- Balsamic glaze for drizzling
- Extra-virgin olive oil for drizzling
- Salt and pepper to taste
- Wooden skewers

Instructions:

1. After rinsing, wipe dry the cherry tomatoes.
2. If necessary, drain the fresh mozzarella balls.
3. Gather new basil leaves straight from the stalks.
4. Thread a cherry tomato, a fresh mozzarella ball, and a fresh basil leaf onto a wooden skewer. Continue until all skewers are stuffed.

5. Put the caprese skewers on a plate for serving.

6. Drizzle the skewers with extra virgin olive oil and balsamic glaze.

7. Season with pepper and salt to taste.

8. Serve these delicious Caprese Skewers with Cherry Tomatoes and Mozzarella right away for a bright and colorful snack or appetizer!

10. Edamame with Sea Salt

Ingredients:

- 1 pound frozen edamame in the pod
- Sea salt, to taste

Instructions:

1. Place a saucepan of water over high heat and bring it to a boil.

2. Pour the boiling water over the frozen edamame pods.

3. Cook the edamame pods for four to five minutes, or until they are soft and well-cooked.

4. Empty the cooked edamame pods onto a serving dish after draining.

5. Lightly toss the edamame pods in the sea salt to get a uniform coating. Sea salt enhances flavor

without adding excessive amounts of sodium, which is beneficial for renal health.

6. You may serve the edamame warm or at room temperature with sea salt.

11. Trail Mix with Nuts and Dried Fruit

Ingredients:

- 1 cup almonds
- 1 cup walnuts
- 1 cup cashews
- 1 cup dried cranberries
- 1 cup raisins
- 1/2 cup pumpkin seeds (pepitas)
- 1/2 cup sunflower seeds
- 1/2 cup dried apricots, chopped

Instructions:

1. Put all the ingredients (almonds, walnuts, cashews, raisins, dried cranberries, pumpkin seeds, sunflower seeds, and dried apricots) in a big bowl.
2. Gently toss the mixture to spread the dry fruits and nuts equally.

3. To make trail mix easier to grab-and-go, split it up into smaller snack packs or store it in an airtight container.
4. Savor the trail mix as a filling midday snack or as a rapid energy boost while engaging in outdoor activities.

This trail mix is a wholesome and kidney-friendly snack choice since it has a decent ratio of protein, fiber, healthy fats, and vitamins. Just monitor the portion sizes, particularly if you're trying to limit your consumption of salt and potassium. Enjoy!

12. Cottage Cheese with Pineapple Rings

Ingredients:

- 1 cup cottage cheese (low-fat or non-fat, if preferred)
- 4 pineapple rings (fresh or canned in juice, drained)

Instructions:

1. Transfer one cup of cottage cheese onto a dish for serving.

2. Surround the cottage cheese with rings of fresh pineapple.

3. Enjoy this easy and energizing cottage cheese with pineapple rings for breakfast or as a quick and healthful snack! Serve right away!

Delicious Desserts and Treats For Seniors

1. Mixed Berry Parfait

Ingredients:

- 1 cup Greek yogurt
- 1 cup mixed berries (strawberries, blueberries, raspberries)
- 1/4 cup granola
- 1 tablespoon honey (optional)
- Mint leaves for garnish

Instructions:

1. Place a layer of 1/4 cup Greek yogurt on the bottom of a glass or serving bowl.
2. Top the yogurt with a layer of mixed berries.
3. Drizzle the berries with a spoonful of granola.
4. Continue layering until the bowl or glass is full.
5. You may optionally sprinkle some honey on top to make it sweeter.
6. Add mint leaves as a garnish.
7. Present the Mixed Berry Parfait right away, and savor this tasty and nourishing dessert!

2. Dark Chocolate-Dipped Strawberries

Ingredients:

- Fresh strawberries, washed and dried
- Dark chocolate chips or chopped dark chocolate (at least 70% cocoa)
- **Optional toppings:** chopped nuts, shredded coconut, sprinkles, sea salt flakes, etc.

Instructions:

1. Line a baking pan with parchment paper or wax.
2. In a heatproof dish over a double boiler or in 30-second microwave bursts, melt the chopped dark chocolate or dark chocolate chips, stirring until smooth.
3. Holding each strawberry by its stem, dip it into the melted chocolate, turning it so that about two-thirds of the fruit is covered.
4. Transfer the coated strawberry to the prepared baking sheet, allowing any excess chocolate to fall off.
5. After the strawberries have been dipped, sprinkle your favorite toppings over them while the chocolate is still wet.

6. Repeat the dipping process with the remaining strawberries.

7. Put the baking sheet in the refrigerator for a half hour to two hours, or until the chocolate solidifies.

8. Transfer the strawberries coated in dark chocolate to a dish or plate after they have solidified.

9. Serve immediately as a delightful snack or dessert.

3. Baked Apples with Cinnamon

Ingredients:

- 4 medium-sized apples (such as Granny Smith or Honeycrisp)
- 2 tablespoons unsalted butter or coconut oil, melted
- 2 tablespoons honey or maple syrup
- 1 teaspoon ground cinnamon
- 1/4 teaspoon ground nutmeg (optional)
- 1/4 cup chopped nuts (such as walnuts or pecans), optional

Instructions:

1. Set the oven temperature to 375°F, or 190°C.

2. Peel and core the apples, keeping the bottoms whole to accommodate the filling, but discarding the seeds and stems.

3. Combine the melted butter or coconut oil, honey, maple syrup, grated nutmeg (if using), and cinnamon in a small bowl.

4. Transfer the cored apples to a baking dish or a parchment paper-lined baking sheet.

5. Fill each apple's hollow by evenly spooning the cinnamon mixture into the middle.

6. Top each stuffed apple with chopped nuts, if you'd like.

7. Bake for 25 to 30 minutes in a preheated oven, or until the filling is bubbling and caramelized and the apples are soft.

8. Before serving, take the baked apples out of the oven and let them cool somewhat.

9. You may alternatively serve the hot Baked Apples with Cinnamon with a scoop of vanilla ice cream or a dab of yogurt.

4. Chia Seed Pudding with Mango

Ingredients:

- 1/4 cup chia seeds
- 1 cup almond milk (or any preferred milk)

- 1 tablespoon honey or maple syrup
- 1/2 teaspoon vanilla extract
- Fresh mango slices for topping

Instructions:

1. Put almond milk, honey (or maple syrup), vanilla essence, and chia seeds in a bowl.
2. Make sure the chia seeds are fully mixed into the mixture by giving it a good stir.
3. To avoid clumping, whisk the mixture once more after letting it settle for about five minutes.
4. To enable the chia seeds to absorb the liquid and take on the consistency of pudding, cover the bowl and refrigerate for at least two hours or overnight.
5. Give the chia seed pudding a thorough stir when it has set.
6. Ladle pudding into jars or serving dishes.
7. Add slices of fresh mango on top.
8. Present the cooled Chia Seed Pudding with Mango and savor this wholesome and delectable dessert or brunch choice!

5. Greek Yogurt with Honey and Nuts

Ingredients:

- 1 cup Greek yogurt (low-fat or non-fat, if preferred)
- 1-2 tablespoons honey, to taste
- 2 tablespoons chopped nuts (such as almonds, walnuts, or pecans)
- Optional toppings: fresh berries, sliced banana, granola

Instructions:

1. Spoon the Greek yogurt into a serving bowl.
2. Drizzle the honey over the Greek yogurt, adjusting the amount to your desired level of sweetness.
3. Sprinkle the chopped nuts over the honey-drizzled yogurt.
4. If desired, add additional toppings such as fresh berries, sliced banana, or granola for extra flavor and texture.
5. Serve the Greek Yogurt with Honey and Nuts immediately and enjoy!

6. Frozen Banana Bites

Ingredients:

- 2 ripe bananas
- 1/4 cup peanut butter (or almond butter)
- Dark chocolate chips
- Chopped nuts (optional)
- Shredded coconut (optional)

Instructions:

1. Cut the ripe bananas into bite-sized pieces after peeling them.
2. Top each banana chunk with a tiny dollop of peanut butter.
3. Press two banana chunks together with their peanut butter sides facing each other to make banana sandwiches.
4. After lining a pan with parchment paper, place the banana sandwiches on it and freeze for at least half an hour.
5. Melt the dark chocolate chips in 20-second bursts in a microwave-safe dish, stirring in between to ensure smoothness.
6. Make sure the frozen banana sandwiches are well covered by dipping them into the melting chocolate.
7. You may optionally top the chocolate-covered banana bites with chopped nuts or shredded coconut.
8. Return the covered banana bites to the parchment paper and freeze for a further thirty minutes, or until the chocolate sets.

9. After the frozen banana bits are completely solid, move them to a container and freeze.

10. Present and savor these tasty and nutritious frozen desserts!

7. Peach Sorbet

Ingredients:

- 4 ripe peaches, peeled, pitted, and chopped
- 1/4 cup honey or maple syrup (adjust to taste)
- 1 tablespoon freshly squeezed lemon juice
- 1/2 teaspoon vanilla extract
- Optional: mint leaves for garnish

Instructions:

1. Fill a food processor or blender with the diced peaches.

2. Fill the blender with the lemon juice, vanilla essence, and honey or maple syrup.

3. Process the mixture until it's creamy and smooth.

4. Taste the sorbet mixture and, if necessary, add additional honey or maple syrup to balance the sweetness.

5. Spoon the sorbet mixture onto a baking pan or shallow dish.

6. To prevent ice crystals from forming, cover the dish with plastic wrap and freeze it for at least 4 hours, or until hard. Stir from time to time.

7. After the sorbet is solid, take it out of the freezer and let it come to room temperature for a little while before serving.

8. Transfer the peach sorbet into serving plates or bowls.

9. If preferred, garnish with fresh mint leaves.

10. Present right away and savor!

8. Almond Flour Blueberry Muffins

Ingredients:

- 2 cups almond flour
- 1/4 cup coconut flour
- 1/2 teaspoon baking soda
- 1/4 teaspoon salt
- 3 large eggs
- 1/4 cup melted coconut oil or melted butter
- 1/3 cup honey or maple syrup
- 1 teaspoon vanilla extract
- 1 cup fresh blueberries

Instructions:

1. Set the oven's temperature to 175°C/350°F. Grease the cups or use paper liners to line a muffin pan.

2. Combine the almond flour, coconut flour, baking soda, and salt in a large basin.

3. Beat the eggs in another basin. Add the vanilla essence, honey, or maple syrup, and melted coconut oil (or butter). Blend well.

4. Transfer the wet ingredients into the dry ingredient dish. Mix until barely incorporated.

5. Make sure the fresh blueberries are uniformly dispersed throughout the batter by gently folding them in.

6. Using a spoon, scoop out the batter and fill each muffin cup approximately two thirds of the way.

7. Bake for 20 to 25 minutes, or until a toothpick inserted into the middle of a muffin comes out clean, in a preheated oven.

8. After letting the muffins cool in the muffin tray for a few minutes, move them to a wire rack to finish cooling.

9. After they're cold, serve and savor these moist and flavorful Almond Flour Blueberry Muffins!

9. Coconut Rice Pudding

Ingredients:

- 1 cup jasmine rice
- 1 can (13.5 oz) coconut milk
- 2 cups milk (or almond milk for a dairy-free option)
- 1/4 cup sugar
- 1 teaspoon vanilla extract
- Pinch of salt
- **Optional toppings:** toasted coconut flakes, sliced almonds, diced mango or pineapple, cinnamon

Instructions:

1. Use cold water to rinse the jasmine rice until the water runs clear. This keeps the rice from getting too sticky and helps get rid of extra starch.
2. Place the washed rice, coconut milk, milk, sugar, vanilla essence, and a little amount of salt in a medium-sized pot.
3. Set the pot on medium heat and, while stirring from time to time, bring the mixture to a mild boil.
4. After bringing the mixture to a boil, lower the heat to a simmer, cover the pot, and cook, stirring from time to time, until the rice is tender and the sauce thickens to the consistency of pudding, about 30 to 35 minutes.
5. Turn off the heat and let the rice pudding cook gently in the pot.

6. You may serve the Coconut Rice Pudding warm or cold, topped with chopped pineapple or mango, sliced almonds, toasted coconut flakes, or a dash of cinnamon.

10. Baked Cinnamon Pears

Ingredients:

- 4 ripe but firm pears, halved and cored
- 2 tablespoons melted butter or coconut oil
- 2 tablespoons honey or maple syrup
- 1 teaspoon ground cinnamon
- 1/4 teaspoon ground nutmeg
- A pinch of salt
- Chopped nuts (optional, for garnish)
- Greek yogurt or vanilla ice cream (optional, for serving)

Instructions:

1. Turn the oven on to 375°F, or 190°C.
2. Split the pears in half, then take out the cores.
3. Combine honey or maple syrup with melted butter or coconut oil in a small bowl.
4. Arrange the pear halves, cut side up, in a baking dish.

5. Drizzle the pears with the melted butter or coconut oil mixture.

6. Combine ground nutmeg, ground cinnamon, and a little amount of salt in another dish. Evenly distribute this mixture on top of the pears.

7. Bake the pears for 25 to 30 minutes, or until they are soft and golden, in a preheated oven.

8. For an optional textural boost, add chopped nuts as a garnish.

9. For a delicious dessert, serve the baked cinnamon pears warm and think about eating them with a scoop of vanilla ice cream or a dollop of Greek yogurt. Have fun!

11. Avocado Chocolate Mousse

Ingredients:

- 2 ripe avocados
- 1/4 cup cocoa powder
- 1/4 cup maple syrup or honey
- 1 teaspoon vanilla extract
- Pinch of salt
- **Optional toppings**: sliced strawberries, raspberries, shaved dark chocolate, chopped nuts

Instructions:

1. Halve the avocados, remove the pits, and transfer the flesh to a food processor or blender.

2. Fill the blender with the cocoa powder, vanilla extract, honey, or maple syrup, and a dash of salt.

3. Blend the ingredients until they are smooth and creamy, stopping the blender occasionally to scrape down the sides to make sure everything is thoroughly mixed in.

4. Taste the chocolate mousse and, if required, add additional honey or maple syrup to balance the sweetness.

5. Spoon the chocolate mousse into glasses or serving dishes.

6. To chill and firm up the mousse, cover the bowls or glasses with plastic wrap and place them in the refrigerator for at least half an hour.

7. After the avocado chocolate mousse has chilled, top it with your preferred toppings, such chopped nuts, shaved dark chocolate, strawberries, or raspberries.

8. Present and savor this decadent but nutritious dessert!

12. Orange Sorbet with Mint

Ingredients:

- 4 large oranges, juiced (about 2 cups)
- 1/2 cup sugar
- 1/2 cup water
- Fresh mint leaves for garnish

Instructions:

1. Put the water and sugar in a saucepan. Stir the sugar and heat over medium heat until it dissolves completely. Let chill the simple syrup.
2. Use the juicer to extract enough fresh orange juice for around two cups.
3. Combine the fresh orange juice and the cooled simple syrup in a basin.
4. Transfer the orange mixture to an ice cream machine and process as directed by the manufacturer.
5. Transfer the sorbet to a container with a cover and freeze it for at least 4 hours, or until it becomes solid, until it reaches a soft-serve consistency.
6. Add some fresh mint leaves as a garnish to the Orange Sorbet.
7. Savor this zesty and cool delicacy as a nice way to clear your palette or as a light dessert!

Quick and Tasty Smoothie Recipes For Seniors After Transplant

1. Berry Blast Smoothie

Ingredients:

- 1 cup mixed berries (such as strawberries, blueberries, raspberries)

- 1 ripe banana
- 1/2 cup plain Greek yogurt (or dairy-free yogurt for a vegan option)
- 1/2 cup spinach leaves (optional, for added nutrition)
- 1/2 cup almond milk (or any milk of your choice)
- 1 tablespoon honey or maple syrup (optional, for added sweetness)
- Ice cubes (optional, for a colder smoothie)

Instructions:

1. Fill a blender with all the ingredients.
2. Blend until creamy and smooth, stopping the blender occasionally to scrape down the sides to make sure everything is completely blended.
3. After tasting the smoothie, taste it again and, if needed, add additional honey or maple syrup to make it more sweet.
4. Add extra frozen berries or bananas for a thicker consistency. Add additional almond milk if you'd want a thinner consistency.
5. Transfer the Berry Blast Smoothie into glasses and serve right away after blending until the desired consistency is reached.
6. If preferred, garnish with more berries or a sprig of mint.

2. Green Powerhouse Smoothie

Ingredients:

- 1 cup spinach leaves
- 1/2 cucumber, peeled and sliced
- 1/2 avocado, peeled and pitted
- 1/2 banana
- 1/2 cup pineapple chunks (fresh or frozen)
- 1 tablespoon chia seeds
- 1 cup unsweetened almond milk (or any preferred milk)
- Ice cubes (optional)

Instructions:

1. Put the spinach leaves, chia seeds, avocado, banana, pineapple pieces, cucumber slices, and spinach into a blender.
2. Add almond milk without added sugar.
3. Blend until creamy and smooth. If you want a cooler consistency, add ice cubes.
4. Fill a glass with the Green Powerhouse Smoothie.
5. You may optionally add more chia seeds or a cucumber slice as a garnish.
6. Savor this nutrient-rich, revitalizing Green Powerhouse Smoothie as a healthy beverage!

3. Tropical Paradise Smoothie

Ingredients:

- 1 ripe banana, frozen
- 1/2 cup frozen pineapple chunks
- 1/2 cup frozen mango chunks
- 1/2 cup coconut milk (or any milk of your choice)
- 1/4 cup Greek yogurt (or dairy-free yogurt for a vegan option)
- 1 tablespoon shredded coconut (optional)
- 1 tablespoon honey or maple syrup (optional, for added sweetness)
- Juice of 1/2 lime (optional, for added tanginess)
- Ice cubes (optional, for a colder smoothie)

Instructions:

1. Fill a blender with all the ingredients.
2. Blend until creamy and smooth, adding more coconut milk or ice cubes as necessary to modify the consistency.
3. After tasting the smoothie, taste it again and, if needed, add additional honey or maple syrup to make it more sweet.
4. Add the juice of half a lime and mix once more for a tart twist.

5. Transfer the Tropical Paradise Smoothie into glasses and serve right away after blending until the appropriate sweetness and consistency are reached.
6. If desired, put some shredded coconut over top as a garnish.

4. Peach and Oat Smoothie

Ingredients:

- 1 cup frozen or fresh peach slices
- 1/2 cup rolled oats
- 1/2 cup Greek yogurt
- 1 tablespoon honey
- 1/2 teaspoon vanilla extract
- 1 cup almond milk (or any preferred milk)
- Ice cubes (optional)

Instructions:

1. Put rolled oats, Greek yogurt, honey, vanilla essence, frozen or fresh peach pieces, and yogurt in a blender.
2. Add the almond milk.
3. Blend until creamy and smooth. If you want your consistency cooler, add some ice cubes.
4. After tasting the smoothie, add additional honey if necessary to regulate the sweetness.

5. Fill a glass with the Peach and Oat Smoothie.

6. You can choose to add an oat sprinkle or a piece of peach as a garnish.

7. Savor this tasty and satisfying Peach and Oat Smoothie for a wholesome morning or midday snack!

5. *Banana Nut Smoothie*

Ingredients:

- 1 ripe banana
- 1/4 cup rolled oats
- 1 tablespoon almond butter (or peanut butter)
- 1/2 cup Greek yogurt (or dairy-free yogurt for a vegan option)
- 1/2 cup almond milk (or any milk of your choice)
- 1 tablespoon honey or maple syrup (optional, for added sweetness)
- 1/2 teaspoon ground cinnamon (optional, for added flavor)
- Ice cubes (optional, for a colder smoothie)

Instructions:

1. Cut the ripe banana into bits after peeling it.
2. Fill a blender with all the ingredients.

3. Blend until creamy and smooth, adding more almond milk or ice cubes as necessary to alter the consistency.

4. After tasting the smoothie, taste it again and add additional honey or maple syrup if needed to make it more sweet.

5. Add ground cinnamon to the blender and pulse once more to add even more flavor.

6. Transfer the banana nut smoothie into glasses and serve right away after blending until the smoothness and sweetness are as you'd like.

7. You can choose to add chopped nuts or a sprinkling of cinnamon as a garnish.

6. Refreshing Watermelon Smoothie

Ingredients:

- 2 cups fresh watermelon, diced and deseeded
- 1 cup cucumber, peeled and chopped
- 1/2 lime, juiced
- 1 tablespoon fresh mint leaves
- 1 cup coconut water
- Ice cubes (optional)

Instructions:

1. Put diced cucumber, lime juice, mint leaves, and fresh watermelon in a blender.

2. Add the coconut water.

3. Process until smooth. If you want a cooler consistency, add ice cubes.

4. After tasting the smoothie, taste and add more lime or mint if desired.

5. Fill a glass with the Refreshing Watermelon Smoothie.

6. For an added touch, garnish with a cucumber slice or a sprig of mint.

7. Savor this energizing and hydrating smoothie as a cool beverage on a hot day!

7. Mango Tango Smoothie

Ingredients:

- 1 ripe mango, peeled and diced (or 1 cup frozen mango chunks)
- 1/2 cup plain Greek yogurt (or dairy-free yogurt for a vegan option)
- 1/2 cup orange juice (freshly squeezed or store-bought)
- 1/2 cup pineapple chunks (fresh or frozen)
- 1 tablespoon honey or maple syrup (optional, for added sweetness)

- Juice of 1/2 lime (optional, for added tanginess)
- Ice cubes (optional, for a colder smoothie)

Instructions:

1. Fill a blender with all the ingredients.
2. Blend until creamy and smooth, adding more orange juice or ice cubes as necessary to modify the consistency.
3. After tasting the smoothie, taste it again and, if needed, add additional honey or maple syrup to make it more sweet.
4. Add the juice of half a lime to the blender and blend once more for an additional burst of acid.
5. Transfer the mango-tango smoothie into glasses and serve right away after blending until the required sweetness and consistency are reached.
6. You can choose to adorn the glass's rim with a mango slice or a lime twist.

8. Cocoa Almond Delight Smoothie

Ingredients:

- 1 banana
- 2 tablespoons almond butter
- 1 tablespoon unsweetened cocoa powder

- 1 cup almond milk (or any preferred milk)
- 1/2 teaspoon vanilla extract
- 1 tablespoon chia seeds
- Ice cubes (optional)

Instructions:

1. Put a ripe banana, almond butter, almond milk, vanilla extract, unsweetened chocolate powder, and chia seeds in a blender.
2. If you like your consistency cooler, add some ice cubes.
3. Blend until creamy and smooth.
4. Fill a glass with the Cocoa Almond Delight Smoothie.
5. For more texture, feel free to add a handful of chia seeds on top.
6. Savor this decadent and healthful Cocoa Almond Delight Smoothie as a delightful dessert!

9. Pineapple Coconut Cooler Smoothie

Ingredients:

- 1 cup frozen pineapple chunks
- 1/2 cup coconut milk

- 1/2 cup plain Greek yogurt (or dairy-free yogurt for a vegan option)
- 1/4 cup orange juice (freshly squeezed or store-bought)
- 1 tablespoon honey or maple syrup (optional, for added sweetness)
- Juice of 1/2 lime (optional, for added tanginess)
- Ice cubes (optional, for a colder smoothie)
- Shredded coconut for garnish (optional)

Instructions:

1. Fill a blender with all the ingredients.
2. Blend until creamy and smooth, adding more coconut milk or ice cubes as necessary to modify the consistency.
3. After tasting the smoothie, taste it again and, if needed, add additional honey or maple syrup to make it more sweet.
4. Add the juice of half a lime to the blender and mix once more for an additional burst of acid.
5. Transfer the Pineapple Coconut Cooler Smoothie into glasses after blending until the desired sweetness and consistency are reached.
6. For an extra touch of tropical flare, you can choose to sprinkle some shredded coconut on top.

10. Strawberry Kiwi Bliss Smoothie

Ingredients:

- 1 cup fresh strawberries, hulled
- 2 kiwi fruits, peeled and sliced
- 1 banana
- 1/2 cup Greek yogurt
- 1 tablespoon honey
- 1 cup coconut water
- Ice cubes (optional)

Instructions:

1. Put ripe banana, Greek yogurt, honey, sliced kiwi fruits, and fresh strawberries in a blender.
2. Add the coconut water.
3. If you want the consistency to be cooler, add ice cubes.
4. Blend until velvety and creamy.
5. Taste the smoothie and, if necessary, add additional honey to balance the sweetness.
6. Fill a glass with the Strawberry Kiwi Bliss Smoothie.
7. For a pretty presentation, top with a whole strawberry or a slice of kiwi.
8. Treat yourself to this tasty and revitalizing Strawberry Kiwi Bliss Smoothie as a lovely drink!

CHAPTER FIVE

SEVEN DAY NUTRITIOUS MEAL PLAN FOR SENIORS AFTER KIDNEY TRANSPLANT SURGERY

Day 1:

- *Breakfast: Berry Bliss Smoothie Bowl*

Ingredients:

- 1/2 cup mixed berries (such as strawberries, blueberries, and raspberries), frozen
- 1/2 ripe banana, frozen
- 1/4 cup plain Greek yogurt (low-fat or non-fat)
- 1/4 cup unsweetened almond milk (or any milk of choice)
- 1 tablespoon chia seeds
- 1 tablespoon honey (optional)
- **Toppings:** sliced strawberries, blueberries, raspberries, granola, sliced almonds, shredded coconut

Instructions:

1. Put the frozen banana, Greek yogurt, chia seeds, almond milk, mixed berries, and honey (if using) in a blender.

2. Blend until creamy and smooth, adding extra almond milk as necessary to get the right consistency.

3. Transfer the blended drink to a bowl.

4. You may add granola, sliced almonds, shredded coconut, strawberries, blueberries, raspberries, or any other toppings you choose on top.

5. Present right away and savor with a spoon.

- Lunch: Grilled Chicken Salad with Fresh Berries

Ingredients:

- 2 boneless, skinless chicken breasts
- Salt and pepper to taste
- 6 cups mixed salad greens (such as spinach, arugula, and romaine)
- 1 cup mixed fresh berries (such as strawberries, blueberries, and raspberries)
- 1/4 cup sliced almonds, toasted
- 1/4 cup crumbled feta cheese (optional)
- Balsamic vinaigrette dressing (homemade or store-bought), to taste

Instructions:

1. Turn the heat up to medium-high on your grill.

2. To taste, add salt and pepper to the chicken breasts.

3. Cook the chicken breasts on the grill for 6 to 8 minutes on each side, or until they are cooked through and no longer have a pink core. Depending on the thickness of the chicken breasts, cooking times might change. After they are done, take them from the grill and give them some time to rest before slicing.

4. Combine the mixed salad greens, sliced almonds, and a variety of fresh berries in a big bowl.

5. After grilling, cut the chicken breasts into slices and place them over the salad.

6. Top the salad with the crumbled feta cheese, if using.

7. Toss the salad gently to coat after adding a drizzle of balsamic vinaigrette dressing, to taste.

8. Enjoy your Grilled Chicken Salad with Fresh Berries right away after serving.

- *Dinner: Baked Herb-Crusted Salmon with Asparagus*

Ingredients:

- 4 salmon filets (about 6 ounces each)

- 1 bunch asparagus, woody ends trimmed
- 2 tablespoons olive oil
- 2 cloves garlic, minced
- Zest of 1 lemon
- Juice of 1 lemon
- 1 tablespoon chopped fresh parsley
- 1 tablespoon chopped fresh dill
- 1 tablespoon chopped fresh thyme
- Salt and pepper to taste
- Lemon slices for garnish

Instructions:

Set the oven temperature to 400°F, or 200°C. Cover a baking sheet with foil or parchment paper.

2. Arrange the salmon filets, allowing space between each one, on half of the baking sheet that has been prepared.

3. Make sure the asparagus spears are arranged in a single layer on the opposite side of the baking sheet.

4. Combine the olive oil, minced garlic, zest and juice of the lemon, chopped parsley, chopped dill, and chopped thyme in a small bowl.

5. Use your hands or a brush to evenly cover the salmon filets and asparagus after drizzling them with the herb mixture.

6. Add salt and pepper to taste and season the asparagus and salmon filets.

7. For added taste, place slices of lemon over the salmon filets.

8. Bake for 12 to 15 minutes in a preheated oven, or until the asparagus is crisp-tender and the salmon is cooked through and flakes readily with a fork.

9. After the salmon and asparagus are done, take the baking sheet out of the oven and allow them to rest for a few minutes before serving.

10. Garnish the baked herb-crusted salmon with lemon slices or more fresh herbs, if you'd like, and serve it hot with asparagus.

Day 2:

- *Breakfast: Greek Yogurt Parfait with Nuts and Honey*

Ingredients:

- 1 cup low-fat Greek yogurt
- 2 tablespoons chopped almonds or walnuts (choose lower phosphorus nuts)
- 1 tablespoon honey

- 1/4 cup fresh berries (blueberries or strawberries work well)
- 1 tablespoon ground flaxseeds (optional)
- 1/2 teaspoon vanilla extract (optional)

Instructions:

1. Spoon a layer of Greek yogurt into the bottom of a serving glass or dish.
2. Top the yogurt with a layer of fresh berries.
3. Top the berries with chopped almonds.
4. Pour honey on top of the fruit and almonds.
5. Continue layering until you reach the top, then sprinkle more honey on top.
6. For added taste, feel free to add a small amount of vanilla essence.
7. For extra nutritious advantages, if preferred, top with ground flaxseeds.
8. Serve right away and savor this tasty and kidney-friendly Greek yogurt parfait!

- *Lunch: Mushroom and Spinach Frittata*

Ingredients:

- 6 large eggs- 1 cup fresh spinach leaves, chopped

- 1 cup mushrooms, sliced
- 1/2 cup low-fat feta cheese, crumbled
- 1/4 cup red onion, finely chopped
- 1 clove garlic, minced
- 1 tablespoon olive oil
- Salt and pepper to taste
- Fresh herbs for garnish (such as parsley or chives)

Instructions:

1. Turn the oven on to 375°F, or 190°C.
2. Beat the eggs well in a basin. Add pepper and salt for seasoning.
3. In an oven-safe skillet, preheat the olive oil over medium heat.
4. Fill the pan with minced garlic and finely chopped red onion. Sauté the food until it becomes tender.
5. Place the sliced mushrooms in the skillet and heat them through, releasing their moisture and turning soft.
6. Add the chopped spinach and heat, stirring, until it wilts.
7. Cover the veggies in the skillet with the beaten eggs.
8. Evenly distribute the feta cheese crumbles on top of the egg mixture.
9. Cook until the edges firm, a few minutes on the heat.

10. Place the pan in the oven that has been warmed, and bake for 15 to 20 minutes, or until the frittata is set through.

11. After cooking, take it out of the oven and give it some time to cool.

12. Cut into wedges and garnish with fresh herbs.

- *Dinner: Vegetable Stir-Fry with Tofu and Brown Rice*

Ingredients:

- 1 block (14-16 ounces) firm tofu, pressed and cubed
- 2 cups cooked brown rice
- 2 tablespoons soy sauce (low-sodium if preferred)
- 1 tablespoon sesame oil
- 2 tablespoons vegetable oil, divided
- 2 cloves garlic, minced
- 1 tablespoon minced ginger
- 1 small onion, thinly sliced
- 2 cups mixed vegetables (such as bell peppers, broccoli, snap peas, carrots), chopped
- 1 cup sliced mushrooms
- Salt and pepper to taste
- **Optional garnish**: chopped green onions, sesame seeds

Instructions:

1. Heat one tablespoon of vegetable oil in a big pan or wok over medium heat.
2. Add the cubed tofu to the skillet and cook for 5 to 7 minutes, or until golden brown on both sides. After taking the tofu out of the skillet, set it aside.
3. Add the last tablespoon of vegetable oil to the same skillet.
4. Add the finely chopped ginger and garlic to the pan and heat for approximately one minute, or until aromatic.
5. Add the sliced onion to the skillet and simmer for three to four minutes, or until softened.
6. Cook for a further five to seven minutes, or until the veggies are crisp-tender, after stirring in the mixed vegetables and sliced mushrooms.
7. Add the cooked brown rice to the skillet along with the tofu that has been cooked.
8. Pour the rice, veggies, and tofu with the soy sauce and sesame oil, then combine everything until it's well covered.
9. To taste, add salt and pepper for seasoning.
10. Cook, stirring periodically, for a further two to three minutes, or until everything is well cooked.
11. Take off the heat and, if you'd like, top with chopped green onions and sesame seeds.

12. Plate the hot vegetable stir-fry with brown rice and tofu, and savor!

Day 3:

- Breakfast: Mango Tango Smoothie

Ingredients:

- 1 ripe mango, peeled and diced (or 1 cup frozen mango chunks)
- 1/2 cup plain Greek yogurt (or dairy-free yogurt for a vegan option)
- 1/2 cup orange juice (freshly squeezed or store-bought)
- 1/2 cup pineapple chunks (fresh or frozen)
- 1 tablespoon honey or maple syrup (optional, for added sweetness)
- Juice of 1/2 lime (optional, for added tanginess)
- Ice cubes (optional, for a colder smoothie)

Instructions:

1. Fill a blender with all the ingredients.

2. Blend until creamy and smooth, adding more orange juice or ice cubes as necessary to modify the consistency.

3. After tasting the smoothie, taste it again and, if needed, add additional honey or maple syrup to make it more sweet.

4. Add the juice of half a lime to the blender and blend once more for an additional burst of acid.

5. Transfer the mango-tango smoothie into glasses and serve right away after blending until the required sweetness and consistency are reached.

6. You can choose to adorn the glass's rim with a mango slice or a lime twist.

- *Lunch: Turkey and Quinoa Stuffed Bell Peppers*

Ingredients:

- 4 large bell peppers, halved and seeds removed
- 1 cup quinoa, rinsed
- 2 cups low-sodium chicken or vegetable broth
- 1 tablespoon olive oil
- 1 onion, finely chopped
- 2 cloves garlic, minced
- 1 pound ground turkey
- 1 can (14 oz) diced tomatoes, drained

- 1 teaspoon ground cumin
- 1 teaspoon smoked paprika
- Salt and pepper to taste
- 1 cup black beans, drained and rinsed
- 1 cup corn kernels (fresh or frozen)
- 1 cup shredded cheese (cheddar or Mexican blend)
- Fresh cilantro for garnish (optional)

Instructions:

1. Start by getting the quinoa ready. After washing one cup of quinoa, simmer it in two cups of vegetable or low-sodium chicken broth. Cook the quinoa and absorb the liquid by simmering it. Put it away.

2. Set the oven temperature to 375°F, or 190°C. Make sure to remove the seeds and membranes by cutting four big bell peppers in half lengthwise.

3. Heat one tablespoon of olive oil in a big pan over medium heat. Finely chop an onion and sauté it until it becomes tender. To unleash the flavors, add two cloves of minced garlic and simmer for a further minute.

4. Add 1 pound of the ground turkey to the skillet, crumble it using a spoon, and heat it until it's deliciously browned. One teaspoon each of ground cumin, smoked paprika, salt, and pepper are used to season the turkey. Add a can of drained chopped

tomatoes and simmer, stirring, for a few minutes, until the flavors meld well.

5. Put the cooked quinoa, one cup of rinsed and drained black beans, one cup of frozen or fresh corn, and the spiced turkey mixture in a big mixing bowl. Make sure the ingredients are thoroughly combined.

6. Transfer the bell pepper halves to a baking tray and stuff the turkey and quinoa mixture into each half to a considerable degree. Sprinkle some shredded cheese (you may use cheddar or a Mexican mix for extra taste) on top of each filled pepper.

7. Bake the baking dish in the preheated oven for about 25 to 30 minutes, or until the peppers are soft, covered with foil.

8. Before serving, top the filled peppers with fresh cilantro if you'd like.

- Dinner: Lentil and Vegetable Stew

Ingredients:

- 1 cup dry green or brown lentils, rinsed and drained
- 1 onion, finely chopped
- 2 carrots, peeled and diced

- 2 celery stalks, diced
- 3 cloves garlic, minced
- 1 can (14 oz) diced tomatoes
- 6 cups vegetable broth
- 1 teaspoon ground cumin
- 1 teaspoon ground coriander
- 1/2 teaspoon smoked paprika
- 1 bay leaf
- Salt and pepper to taste
- 2 cups chopped kale or spinach
- 2 tablespoons olive oil
- Fresh parsley for garnish

Instructions:

1. Heat the olive oil in a big saucepan over medium heat. Add the chopped celery, carrots, and onion. Sauté the veggies till they get tender.
2. Add the minced garlic and cook it for a minute more, or until it becomes aromatic.
3. Add the chopped tomatoes, dried lentils, smoked paprika, bay leaf, vegetable broth, ground cumin, and ground coriander. Season with salt and pepper. Mix well to blend.
4. After bringing the stew to a boil, lower the heat to a simmer, cover it, and let it cook for 25 to 30 minutes, or until the lentils are soft.
5. Stir the chopped spinach or kale into the saucepan until it wilts.

6. Taste and, if necessary, adjust seasoning.

7. Before serving, take out the bay leaf.

8. Spoon the vegetable and lentil stew into individual dishes.

9. Add some fresh parsley as a garnish for a taste and color pop.

10. Present and savor this filling and nutritious lentil and vegetable stew!

Day 4:

- Breakfast: Chia Seed Pudding with Berries

Ingredients:

- 1/4 cup chia seeds
- 1 cup low-fat milk (or a milk substitute like almond milk)
- 1 tablespoon honey or maple syrup
- 1/2 teaspoon vanilla extract
- A pinch of salt
- 1/2 cup mixed berries (blueberries, strawberries, raspberries)

Instructions:

1. Put the low-fat milk, vanilla essence, honey (or maple syrup), chia seeds, and a small amount of salt in a bowl.
2. In order to prevent clumping, carefully whisk the ingredients together.
3. After letting the mixture settle for about five minutes, whisk it once more to remove any remaining chia seed clusters.
4. To enable the chia seeds to absorb the liquid and take on the consistency of pudding, cover the bowl and refrigerate for at least three hours or overnight.
5. To achieve a uniform texture before serving, mix the chia pudding.
6. Ladle the chia pudding into glasses or serving dishes.
7. Sprinkle mixed berries over the pudding.

- *Lunch: Caprese Salad with Balsamic Glaze*

Ingredients:

- 1 cup cherry tomatoes, halved
- 1 cup fresh mozzarella cheese, cubed

- Fresh basil leaves
- 2 tablespoons extra-virgin olive oil
- 2 tablespoons balsamic glaze
- Salt and pepper to taste

Instructions:

1. Arrange fresh mozzarella cubes and split cherry tomatoes on a serving plate.
2. Place a few fresh basil leaves in between the mozzarella and tomatoes.
3. Distribute the extra-virgin olive oil equally across the mozzarella and tomatoes.
4. To taste, add salt and pepper for seasoning.
5. Drizzle the salad with balsamic glaze to finish.
6. Serve right away to let the flavors mingle.

- *Dinner: Baked Teriyaki Chicken with Broccoli*

Ingredients:

For the Teriyaki Chicken:

- 4 boneless, skinless chicken breasts
- 1/2 cup soy sauce (low-sodium if preferred)
- 1/4 cup honey

- 2 tablespoons rice vinegar
- 2 cloves garlic, minced
- 1 teaspoon grated ginger
- 1 tablespoon cornstarch (optional, for thickening)

For the Broccoli:

- 2 heads of broccoli, cut into florets
- 2 tablespoons olive oil
- Salt and pepper to taste

Optional Garnish:

- Sesame seeds
- Sliced green onions

Instructions:

Set the oven temperature to 400°F, or 200°C. For easier cleanup, line a baking sheet with foil or parchment paper.

2. Over medium heat, mix the soy sauce, honey, rice vinegar, grated ginger, and chopped garlic in a small saucepan. Simmer and cook the mixture for two to three minutes.

3. Make a slurry out of the cornstarch and two tablespoons of water if you would like your sauce to be thicker. After adding the slurry to the sauce, heat

it for a further one to two minutes, or until it slightly thickens. Take off the heat and place aside.

4. Transfer the chicken breasts to the baking sheet that has been ready. Transfer half of the teriyaki sauce to the chicken and set aside the remaining half for another time.

5. Bake the chicken for 20 to 25 minutes, or until it's cooked through and the middle is no longer pink, in a preheated oven.

6. Toss the broccoli florets with olive oil, salt, and pepper on a separate baking sheet while the chicken bakes.

7. Put the broccoli in the oven in a single layer and roast it for 15 to 20 minutes, or until it is soft and has a faint browning around the edges.

8. Take the chicken and broccoli out of the oven when they're done.

9. Cover the roasted chicken with the leftover teriyaki sauce.

10. If wanted, top the hot baked teriyaki chicken with broccoli with sliced green onions and sesame seeds.

Day 5:

- *Breakfast: Banana Nut Smoothie*

Ingredients:

- 1 ripe banana
- 1/4 cup rolled oats
- 1 tablespoon almond butter (or peanut butter)
- 1/2 cup Greek yogurt (or dairy-free yogurt for a vegan option)
- 1/2 cup almond milk (or any milk of your choice)
- 1 tablespoon honey or maple syrup (optional, for added sweetness)
- 1/2 teaspoon ground cinnamon (optional, for added flavor)
- Ice cubes (optional, for a colder smoothie)

Instructions:

1. Cut the ripe banana into bits after peeling it.
2. Fill a blender with all the ingredients.
3. Blend until creamy and smooth, adding more almond milk or ice cubes as necessary to alter the consistency.
4. After tasting the smoothie, taste it again and add additional honey or maple syrup if needed to make it more sweet.
5. Add ground cinnamon to the blender and pulse once more to add even more flavor.

6. Transfer the banana nut smoothie into glasses and serve right away after blending until the smoothness and sweetness are as you'd like.

7. You can choose to add chopped nuts or a sprinkling of cinnamon as a garnish.

- *Lunch: Lentil Soup with Spinach and Tomatoes*

Ingredients:

- 1 cup dried lentils, rinsed and drained
- 4 cups low-sodium vegetable broth
- 1 onion, diced
- 2 cloves garlic, minced
- 2 carrots, diced
- 2 stalks celery, diced
- 1 can (14.5 oz) diced tomatoes, undrained
- 2 cups fresh spinach leaves, roughly chopped
- 1 teaspoon dried thyme
- 1 teaspoon dried oregano
- Salt and pepper to taste
- 1 tablespoon olive oil

Instructions:

1. Heat the olive oil in a big saucepan or Dutch oven over medium heat.

2. Include the chopped celery, carrots, onion, and garlic in the saucepan. Simmer for 5 to 7 minutes, or until the veggies are tender, stirring periodically.

3. Fill the saucepan with the dry lentils, vegetable broth, chopped tomatoes (including juice), dried oregano, and dried thyme. Mix everything together.

4. After bringing the soup to a boil, turn down the heat. The lentils should be soft after 20 to 25 minutes of simmering under cover.

5. Add the chopped fresh spinach leaves to the cooked lentils. Cook the spinach for a further two to three minutes, or until it wilts.

6. Add salt and pepper to taste when preparing the soup.

7. Before serving, take the pot off of the burner and allow the soup to cool somewhat.

8. Present the heated Lentil Soup with Spinach and Tomatoes, topped with a dollop of Greek yogurt or a sprinkling of grated Parmesan cheese.

- *Dinner: Mediterranean Chickpea Wrap*

Ingredients:

- 1 whole wheat or low-sodium wrap
- 1/2 cup canned chickpeas, drained and rinsed
- 1 tablespoon olive oil
- 1 clove garlic, minced
- 1/2 teaspoon ground cumin
- 1/2 teaspoon paprika
- Salt and pepper to taste
- 2 tablespoons hummus
- 1/4 cup cucumber, thinly sliced
- 1/4 cup cherry tomatoes, halved
- 1/4 cup red bell pepper, thinly sliced
- 2 tablespoons Kalamata olives, sliced
- 1/4 cup feta cheese, crumbled
- Fresh parsley for garnish (optional)
- Lemon wedges for serving

Instructions:

1. Heat the olive oil in a skillet over medium heat.
2. Once aromatic, add the minced garlic and sauté it for one minute.
3. Fill the skillet with the chickpeas, paprika, ground cumin, salt, and pepper. Cook until chickpeas are brown and spice-coated, about 5 to 7 minutes.
4. Follow the directions on the package to reheat the wrap.
5. Evenly cover the middle of the wrap with hummus.

6. Spoon the hummus into the seasoned chickpeas.

7. Arrange the chopped feta cheese, cherry tomatoes, red bell pepper, cucumber slices, and Kalamata olives on top of the chickpeas.

8. If preferred, garnish with fresh parsley.

9. Tightly roll the wrap by folding its sides.

10. Halve the wrapper lengthwise and present it with lemon wedges beside it.

Day 6:

- *Breakfast: Avocado Toast with Poached Egg*

Ingredients:

- 1 ripe avocado
- 2 slices whole grain bread, toasted
- 2 large eggs
- Salt and pepper to taste
- **Optional toppings:** sliced cherry tomatoes, chopped fresh herbs (such as parsley or chives), red pepper flakes

Instructions:

1. To begin, poach the eggs. Pour some water into a small pot and heat it gently over medium heat.
2. Crack each egg into a ramekin or little dish. Gently place every egg into the water that is simmering. For a soft yolk, cook for 3–4 minutes, or longer if preferred.
3. Cut the avocado in halves and remove the pit while the eggs are poaching. Place the avocado flesh in a bowl and use a fork to mash it until it's smooth. To taste, add salt and pepper for seasoning.
4. Evenly distribute the mashed avocado over the slices of toasted whole grain bread.
5. After the eggs have finished poaching, use a slotted spoon to carefully remove them from the water and drain any extra water.
6. Top each avocado toast with one poached egg.
7. If preferred, garnish with extras like red pepper flakes, chopped fresh herbs, or sliced cherry tomatoes.
8. While the eggs are still warm, serve right away.

- *Lunch: Zucchini Noodles with Pesto and Cherry Tomatoes*

Ingredients:

- 4 medium-sized zucchinis, spiralized into noodles
- 1 cup cherry tomatoes, halved
- 1/2 cup homemade or store-bought pesto sauce
- 2 tablespoons olive oil
- Salt and pepper to taste
- Grated Parmesan cheese for garnish (optional)
- Fresh basil leaves for garnish

Instructions:

1. Using a spiralizer or vegetable peeler, spiralize the zucchini into noodles.
2. Heat the olive oil in a big skillet over medium heat.
3. Add the zucchini noodles to the skillet and cook them for two to three minutes, or until they are slightly crunchy but still soft.
4. Add the cherry tomatoes and continue to sauté for a further one to two minutes, or until the tomatoes are well heated.
5. Add the pesto sauce to the pan and mix the tomatoes and zucchini noodles until they are covered evenly.
6. To taste, add salt and pepper for seasoning. Keep in mind that salt is a common ingredient in pesto.
7. Turn off the heat and place the noodles on serving dishes.

8. For an explosion of flavor, garnish with fresh basil leaves and grated Parmesan cheese, if preferred.
9. Serve right away and savor your tasty and light zucchini noodles with cherry tomatoes and pesto!

- *Dinner: Grilled Veggie and Hummus Wrap*

Ingredients:

- 1 large whole wheat or spinach tortilla
- 1/4 cup hummus (store-bought or homemade)
- 1/2 cup mixed grilled vegetables (such as bell peppers, zucchini, eggplant, and red onion), sliced
- 1/4 cup crumbled feta cheese (optional)
- Handful of baby spinach leaves
- 1 tablespoon olive oil
- Salt and pepper to taste

Instructions:

1. Turn up the heat to medium-high on an outdoor grill or grill pan.
2. Evenly coat the sliced mixed veggies with a mixture of olive oil, salt, and pepper.

3. Grill the veggies until they are soft and have grill marks, 3 to 4 minutes on each side.

4. Place the tortilla in a level, spotless manner.

5. Evenly cover the tortilla with hummus, leaving a thin border all the way around.

6. Evenly distribute the grilled veggies on top of the hummus.

7. Top the veggies with the crumbled feta cheese, if using.

8. Add a few young spinach leaves on top.

9. To create a wrap, fold in the tortilla's sides and then tightly roll it up from the bottom.

10. If preferred, cut the wrap in half diagonally, and serve right away.

Day 7:

- *Breakfast: Protein-Packed Green Smoothie*

Ingredients:

- 1 cup spinach leaves (fresh or frozen)
- 1/2 ripe banana

- 1/2 cup Greek yogurt (plain or vanilla flavored)
- 1/2 cup almond milk (or any milk of your choice)
- 1 tablespoon almond butter or peanut butter
- 1 tablespoon chia seeds or ground flaxseeds
- Optional: 1 scoop of your favorite protein powder
- Ice cubes (optional, for a colder smoothie)

Instructions:

1. Fill a blender with all the ingredients.
2. Blend until creamy and smooth, adding more almond milk or ice cubes as necessary to modify the consistency.
3. After tasting the smoothie, you may add additional banana or, if you'd like, pour some honey or maple syrup to change the sweetness.
4. Transfer the protein-packed green smoothie into glasses after blending until the smoothness and sweetness are as you'd like.
5. Present right away and savor!

- *Lunch: Quinoa and Roasted Vegetable Stuffed Peppers*

Ingredients:

- 4 large bell peppers, halved and seeds removed

- 1 cup quinoa, rinsed
- 2 cups low-sodium vegetable broth or water
- 2 tablespoons olive oil
- 1 small eggplant, diced
- 1 zucchini, diced
- 1 red onion, diced
- 1 red bell pepper, diced
- 2 cloves garlic, minced
- 1 teaspoon dried oregano
- 1 teaspoon dried thyme
- Salt and pepper to taste
- 1/2 cup crumbled feta cheese (optional)
- Fresh parsley for garnish

Instructions:

1. Set the oven's temperature to 400°F, or 200°C.
2. Transfer the split bell peppers to a baking tray and keep them out of the way.
3. Bring water or vegetable broth to a boil in a saucepan. After adding the quinoa, lower the heat, cover, and simmer until the quinoa is cooked and the liquid has been absorbed—about 15 minutes. Using a fork, fluff and set aside.
4. Heat the olive oil in a big pan over medium heat.
5. Fill the skillet with diced eggplant, zucchini, red onion, red bell pepper, and minced garlic. Until the veggies are soft, sauté them.
6. Add salt, pepper, dried thyme, and oregano.

7. Mix the cooked quinoa with the sautéed veggies. Add some crumbled feta cheese if desired.

8. Place the quinoa and roasted veggie mixture into each half of a bell pepper.

9. Bake the baking dish in the preheated oven for 20 to 25 minutes, or until the peppers are soft, covered with foil.

10. Before serving, garnish with fresh parsley.

- Dinner: Eggplant Parmesan with Whole Wheat Pasta

Ingredients:

- 1 large eggplant, sliced into 1/2-inch rounds
- 1 cup whole wheat breadcrumbs
- 2 eggs, beaten
- 2 cups marinara sauce
- 1 cup shredded mozzarella cheese
- 1/2 cup grated Parmesan cheese
- 1 teaspoon dried oregano
- 1 teaspoon dried basil
- Salt and pepper to taste
- 2 tablespoons olive oil
- 8 oz whole wheat pasta, cooked according to package instructions
- Fresh basil leaves for garnish

Instructions:

1. Turn the oven on to 375°F, or 190°C.
2. Combine whole wheat breadcrumbs, salt, pepper, dried oregano, and dried basil in a small basin.
3. Gently press the breadcrumb mixture over the eggplant slices after dipping them into the beaten eggs and making sure they are well covered.
4. Heat the olive oil in a big pan over medium heat. Cook the breaded eggplant slices until golden brown, 2 to 3 minutes each side. After cooking, transfer the slices to a paper towel to drain excess oil.
5. Apply a thin layer of marinara sauce to a baking dish. Arrange the cooked eggplant slices in a single layer on top.
6. Top the eggplant layer with grated Parmesan cheese and shredded mozzarella. Continue layering the ingredients until all are utilized, and then top with a layer of cheese.
7. Bake for 25 to 30 minutes, or until the cheese is bubbling and melted, in a preheated oven.
8. Prepare whole wheat pasta per package directions while the eggplant parmesan bakes.
9. Top whole wheat pasta with the eggplant parmesan.
10. For a splash of freshness, garnish with fresh basil leaves.

11. Savor your tasty and healthful Whole Wheat
Pasta with Eggplant Parmesan!

CHAPTER SIX

COMMON QUESTION ABOUT KIDNEY TRANSPLANT DIETS FOR SENIORS (FAQs)

1. After a kidney transplant, can I still eat the foods I love?

- A lot of favorite meals may be eaten in moderation. But it's crucial to think about how it will affect kidney health and collaborate with medical experts to develop a diet that is both balanced and kidney-friendly.

2. What role does diet have in a kidney transplant's success?

- A healthy diet promotes general well-being, facilitates recovery, and helps avert problems. It is essential to preserving the lifetime and functionality of the kidney transplant.

3. Should I stay away from any certain meals to safeguard my kidney transplant?

Foods high in potassium, phosphorus, and salt may need to be consumed in moderation. Protecting the transplanted kidney involves identifying and limiting certain foods in collaboration with healthcare specialists.

4. What is the suggested protein intake for a diet following kidney transplantation?

While protein is necessary for healing, too much of it might damage the kidneys. The key is moderation and selecting high-quality sources of protein. Everybody has different demands, thus advice from medical professionals is essential.

5. Should salt consumption be restricted following kidney transplantation?

- It is true that reducing salt aids in blood pressure and fluid balance management. A kidney-friendly diet is supported by limiting processed meals and sticking to fresh, natural foods.

6. Are there any limitations on fluids and what part do they play in post-transplant nutrition?

It's important to stay hydrated, but consuming too much fluids might harm your kidneys. Balance is maintained by keeping an eye on fluid intake in accordance with personal requirements and medical guidance.

7. Can I still have snacks and sweets after receiving a kidney transplant?

Yes, as long as you choose your ingredients carefully and in proportion. When adapted to each person's specific nutritional requirements, desserts and snacks can be included in a kidney-friendly diet.

8. Are there any vitamins or supplements I ought to think about consuming?

- Recommendations for supplements such as iron or vitamin D may vary based on personal needs. To prevent possible issues, it is essential to discuss supplement consumption with healthcare specialists.

9. How can I control my weight after having a kidney transplant?

- It's crucial to strike a balance between calorie consumption and exercise. Eating a diet rich in nutrients and well-balanced promotes both weight control and general health.

10. What possible obstacles can one face when following a diet that is kidney-friendly?

- Difficulties might include adjusting to changes in lifestyle, balancing nutritional intake, and dietary limitations. Having regular contact with healthcare providers aids in addressing and resolving these issues.

11. How can I follow dietary limitations and yet add variety to my meals?

Meals may be made more interesting by including a range of fruits, vegetables, lean meats, and nutritious grains. Adding different herbs and spices to food improves taste without endangering kidney function.

12. Are there any particular cooking techniques that recipients of kidney transplants should follow?

- Cooking techniques including baking, grilling, steaming, and sautéing are often good for your kidneys. Meals may be made more nutritious by employing herbs for taste and reducing additional fats.

13. Are there any restrictions on my ability to drink alcohol following a kidney transplant?

- While moderate alcohol use may be permitted, it's important to speak with medical professionals. Customized advice is essential since alcohol can affect renal function and mix with drugs.

14. After receiving a transplant, how frequently should my nutritional status be checked?

- Nutritional status needs to be regularly monitored, particularly in the early post-transplant phase. Healthcare professionals may plan evaluations according to each patient's requirements and medical history.

15. How important is exercise for maintaining health after a kidney transplant?

Frequent exercise is good for your general health and wellbeing after a transplant. It promotes cardiovascular health, aids with weight management, and enhances the post-transplant experience.

CONCLUSION

As we wrap up this extensive book, we take a moment to consider the trip we've been on to help seniors with the post-kidney transplant chapter. For individuals who have had this life-changing treatment, this book serves as a beacon of empowerment, guiding them through the complexities of diet, lifestyle, and thoughtful decisions.

The road after a kidney transplant is an example of adaptability and resilience. Realizing the critical role diet plays is one of the pillars of a good life after transplant. Our research has served as a compass, directing elders toward decisions that support both the body and the transplanted organ, from the delicate balance of proteins to the careful control of sodium, potassium, and phosphorus.

This phase's obstacles are faced with discernment and useful insights. By answering the concerns about hydration management, dietary limitations, and incorporating diversity into meals, we enable seniors to face these obstacles head-on.

Understanding that keeping up a kidney-friendly diet might present challenges, we've offered a road map for doing so, encouraging an optimistic and proactive attitude.

We provide a selection of recipes that have been thoughtfully and purposefully created as we get closer to the finish of our project. All of these recipes—which range from delicious breakfasts to decadent meals, simple snacks to enticing sweets, and cool smoothies—encapsulate the best of both delicious food and kidney-friendly nutrition. Every recipe serves as evidence that one's enjoyment of food and flavor need not be sacrificed after receiving a transplant.

We honor the tenacity of elderly people who have accepted a new chapter in their lives following a kidney transplant as we wrap up our tour. A victory over adversity may be observed in the careful following of dietary guidelines, the dedication to an active lifestyle, and the discernment to take on obstacles head-on.

When seniors start this life-changing adventure, this book is a trusted companion full of knowledge and inspiration. We value tailored treatment and promote constant contact between patients and medical professionals. As we part ways, we really hope that this guide will act as a solid foundation, pointing elders in the direction of long-term health, happiness, and contentment following a kidney transplant.

Made in the USA
Columbia, SC
22 June 2024

671e8aac-1e71-4efd-91ae-398b5fa77ad6R02